# IN THE PURSUIT OF HAPPINESS

FÉLIX VARELA's COLLECTION # 40

EDICIONES UNIVERSAL, Miami, Florida, 2009

P. Ernesto Fernández-Travieso, S.J.

# IN THE PURSUIT
# OF HAPPINESS

Copyright © 2009 by Ernesto Fernández-Travieso, S.J.

———

First edition in Spanish, 2006
First edition in English, 2009

EDICIONES UNIVERSAL
P.O. Box 450353 (Shenandoah Station)
Miami, FL 33245-0353. USA
Tel: (305) 642-3234   Fax: (305) 642-7978
e-mail: ediciones@ediciones.com
http://www.ediciones.com

Library of Congress Catalog Card No.: 2009
ISBN-10: 1-59388-159-2
ISBN-13: 978-1-59388-159-7

Cover design: Luis García Fresquet

Sculpture in the cover: "Free Fall", Robert Cook, Rome
Interior illustration: sculptures by Robert Cook
www.robertcook.org

Photo of the author in the back cover: Don Doll, S.J.

No part of this book
may be reproduced without
writing permission from the author.
For information contact Ediciones Universal.

# INDEX

AUTOBIOGRAPHICAL NOTE .......................... 7

PROLOGUE BY THE AUTHOR ....................... 27

**PART I**
**THE PROBLEM WITH HAPPINESS** ................ 33
    INTRODUCTION ................................. 35
    1)   WHAT HAPPINESS IS NOT .................... 37
    2)   THE PURPOSE OF LIFE ....................... 39
    3)   A HUMANIZING PROCESS THROUGH LIFE ..... 42
    4)   THE SEARCH FOR HAPPINESS IN ANCIENT
           CIVILIZATIONS ............................. 47
    5)   THE GREEKS ................................ 49
    6)   THE BABYLONIANS .......................... 51
    7)   THE HEBREW ............................... 54
    8)   A UNIQUE HISTORICAL DOCUMENT ........... 58
    CONCLUSION PART I ............................ 60

**PART II**
**HISTORY OF THE GROWING HUMAN**
**CONSCIOUSNESS** ................................ 63
    9)   CENTRATION ............................... 67
    10) DECENTRATION ............................. 74
    11) SUPERCENTRATION, SPIRITUAL INTEGRATION 78
    12) SUFFERING AND EVIL ....................... 86
    13) A PREVIEW OF A NEW DIMENSION ............ 96
    14) THE IDEA OF GOD EVOLVING IN JEWISH
           HISTORY ................................... 99
    15) A DEEPER MEANING FOR LIFE ............... 102
    CONCLUSION PART II ........................... 104

**PART III**
**A NEW VISION FOR THE PURPOSE OF LIFE** ....... 109
    16) IN THE FULLNESS OF TIME .................. 111

| 17) | AN ENIGMATIC UNIQUE FIGURE IN HISTORY | 118 |
| 18) | THE MESSAGE FROM A KINGDOM OUT OF THIS WORLD | 123 |
| 19) | A UNIVERSAL ANSWER? | 125 |
| 20) | THE GREAT CONTRADICTION: DYING IN ORDER TO LIVE? | 138 |
| 21) | THE LORD OF FAILURE | 143 |
| 22) | A UNIVERSAL MODEL FOR ALL HUMANITY | 145 |
|     | CONCLUSION PART III | 148 |

**EPILOGUE** .................................................. 157
   A METHOD TO FIND TRUE HAPPINESS ............ 164

**NOTE** ......................................................... 169

**PRINCIPAL BIBLIOGRAPHIC SOURCES** .......... 171

## AUTOBIOGRAPHICAL NOTE

If you want to understand and truly appreciate this book, you must follow my own personal journey in the search for happiness. You must know "where I am coming from."

I was born in Cuba in 1939 and grew up in a family very much aware of the political changes that were happening in my country. Cuba became a Republic very late in 1902 after the independence war, which is unlike most of the other countries in Latin America. They became independent much earlier through the efforts of Bolivar and San Martin. Spain was reluctant to let go of their most developed, productive, and important colony. Because of this, Cuban independence had been very violent and particularly ugly, mainly because Spain, involved the Catholic Church strongly against the independence movement.

Most Cubans, even first generation Spanish descendants, were in favor of the Independence. Additionally, many Cuban born priests were also supporting the independence from the rule of Spain and contrary to the politics of the Catholic Church. This led to persecution, exile, and even deportation to horrid penal colonies. There were even cases of Catholic priests killed in the firing squad with little reaction from the bishops. Catholic Cubans heard in despair of Pope Leo XIII, pressed and misinformed by Spain, blessing the Spanish troops being sent to Cuba to defend Catholic Spain and fight against the Cuban patriots.

Because of this, there was strong animosity toward the Catholic Church among the people in the patriotic movement. The independence efforts and then the new Republic became as a consequence anticlerical. Men seldom participated in Church functions. The liturgies and sacraments were mainly attended by women and children.

Even though my family was Catholic and all members went to Catholic schools, anticlericalism was very strong. My father said he was proud to have never knelt in Church, and for many years he forbade my mother to go to confession.

My paternal grandparents strongly supported the war for independence and directly helped the warriors as they camped in their country property. My grandfather, a pharmacist and his brother, a physician, were providing the warriors with medical attention. As their clandestine activities were discovered by the Spanish, they were sent with their whole families to Isla de Pinos, where a penal colony was established for all who were proved to be connected with the Independence cause. My father, a medical student, had been sent abroad to protect him from the Spanish repression.

When the war was over, my grandparents were honored with medals as veterans of war for their patriotic involvement. These medals, along with the new Cuban flag, were displayed with pride in our living room. I listened attentively as a child to all these stories; especially, from my grandmother, who sat in the afternoons with our extended family to reminisce about the times of the independence. My father finally had returned from exile and graduated from Medical school in 1901 and became a prestigious surgeon.

Even though most families I knew had the same animosity towards religion, especially the men, I always felt disappointed about the way my father felt about religion. I was growing to be a believer in the school with the Christian Brothers. However, I was very proud about my father, a prominent physician, because of the way people loved him and respected him. In his own way, he was a very good Christian who was always helping others in the hospitals, especially the poor. By the way, my father was born in 1876 and was 30 years older than my mother. They met when my mother at 18 contracted typhoid fever. My father, still a bachelor at 48, saved her life. Three years later they were married and had three children.

Back to my country's history, Cuba finally became a free republic in May of 1902 after two years of an obscure intervention by The United States, who participated in the Cuban War for Independence in its final months.

I heard as a child how my maternal grandmother had sewn two large Cuban flags, one for their home, and another for my family home to be displayed on that historical celebration.

Through many political conflicts, Cuba struggled to grow as a free Republic. I grew up listening to the discussions of family and friends of the family, about the different movements and changes. My uncle, on my mother's side was a prominent professor at the 300 year old Universidad de la Habana. In 1940, he participated in the writing of the most progressive Republic Constitution ever written in America.

It was in 1952 when the still young Republic of Cuba fell under the dictatorship of Fulgencio Batista. The intellectual classes and the professionals rejected Batista from the very beginning. At home I listened to the discussions of family and friends about what an insult it was to the Cuban people that this ambitious and uncouth military man would rule the country illegally. Some said that the United States was behind the planning of Batista's "coup d'etat." He was certainly supported and recognized by Washington D.C. immediately upon taking over.

Despite this, Cuba grew to be one of the most economically successful countries in Latin America and in the world, according to the statistics, with one of the highest standards of living and the most extended middle class. Cuban culture was highly European because of the long history of Cuba as a rich Spanish colony. During Napoleon's empire and the French occupation of Spain, Cuba became very French in manners and enjoyed a very high intellectual level. The extended middle class enjoyed that high educational level and European culture.

Nevertheless, there was poverty in Cuba. The situation of slavery, almost until the time of the independence, had created big social adjustments. Slums grew around the big cities and tenement halls invaded the old part of the city of Havana. The countryside was almost forgotten by the new political powers. It seemed that they cared only for the well developed sugar cane industry and not the agricultural development. The "campesinos" were abandoned. Young people went to the cities looking for jobs, but sadly ended being exploited.

Batista was very popular among the poor in the cities. With condescending paternalism to the poor and the campesinos he bragged about the economical development he had achieved and kept making promises. This economical development never filtered down to the poor, but maintained them illusory hopeful and supportive of the government.

Most of the middle class, professionals, and intellectuals were opposed to Batista. Because of this, it did not take long for a political revolution to rally against the illegal dictatorial regime. All adult members in my extended family, although never personally involved in politics, were actively conscious of the different political movements and civic organizations. They were strongly supportive of a revolution against Batista.

I grew up to be a concerned adolescent listening to all these historical developments. I graduated from my private Catholic school when I was sixteen years old, and went to a private Catholic university in Havana. There, some friends invited me to join a very well known Catholic organization directed by the Jesuits. For the first time in my life, I saw adult men receiving communion at Mass. Batista's regime was making us all very aware of the need for a true Christian social consciousness. Through this Catholic organization, I volunteered to teach at a night school for poor workers in a "barrio" on the outskirts of Havana. My life was transformed in many ways. For the first time in my life I came into contact with poverty in my own country and experienced first hand true economic poverty when I visited an impoverished home. One of my students had suffered an accident at work that almost amputated his arm. Without any bitterness he explained to me that his boss sent him to the emergency room at a public hospital and never helped him afterwards even when he lost his job. I was awakening to the reality of my country and getting restless about my responsibility and involvement as a young adult.

This restlessness brought me closer to this Catholic organization. Most of my new friends were getting actively involved in student movements against Batista's dictatorship. I was eighteen and eager to get involved despite my parents' opposition.

We were denouncing the injustices of the system and even the social injustices that oppressed the poor and the rural people throughout the country. Most revolutionary movements against Batista never pronounced themselves beyond political terms. Among these was Fidel Castro's group. His group never mentioned a social revolution, but just the political destitution of Batista's regime.

The year of 1958 was particularly difficult. As a young man I endured the persecution of Batista's repressive forces. In Havana especially, dead bodies of young students appeared on the streets, tortured and assassinated by the police and the paramilitary secret forces of the government.

The last Christmas under Batista, was particularly hard as his repressive forces tried to eliminate any opposition and resistance. All the universities and schools had been closed months before when the dictator declared them centers of dissent and rebellion. No youngster could be found in the streets of Havana after dusk.

At home, we gave shelter to students who were running away and hiding from the police.

Just two days before Batista's fall, four friends of mine, Josè Ignacio "Nacho" Martí, Julio Martinez Inclán, Javier Calvo, and Ramón "Mongo" Rodriguez, from the student Catholic organization where I belonged, were tortured and assassinated by Batista's repressive forces, when trying to join rebels in the western mountain range, not far from Havana.

For many years, the Jesuit Catholic organization where I belonged, had been working quietly developing a new kind of Catholic youth and young professionals organization, through spiritual and intellectual study and reflection. I made, for the first time in my life, a retreat on the Spiritual Exercises of Ignatius of Loyola. I was moved by faith and by the newly found Christian spirit I never knew existed. We studied the new Democratic movements in Europe, Jacques Maritain, Konrad Adenauer, de Gasperi, Sturzo, Fanfani, Cuban and world history, along with the new social Papal Encyclical documents. In 1956, we were outraged when the Soviet tanks got involved with the revolt in Hungary, where many students were killed.

The dictator Batista was finally overthrown on January 1, 1959. We were overjoyed when, early in the morning, we heard that Batista had flown away.

Fidel Castro's group was one among many organizations that participated in the final blow against Batista. He was the most well known Cuban revolutionary because of the large publicity given to him by the New York Times and Life Magazine, especially after the daring coverage those publications conducted up in the mountains. Castro was interviewed as the "romantic" bearded rebel in the mountains, an image that make him an idol all over the world. Castro had his rebel camps in the eastern mountain range about 500 miles far away from Havana.

Castro took over as dictator of Cuba after being accepted with certain apprehension by all the other revolutionary groups. Many people would not trust him for his murky past. Nevertheless, we all cooperated with the new revolution that seemed to open up new horizons to our future. Surprisingly, Castro proclaimed a never ending revolution which was now announcing social changes that specifically interested all of us, typical non-conformists young students. We applauded the changes with enthusiasm.

Surprisingly, some true Christian revolutionary leaders in the newly formed government invited us, Catholic students, to volunteer in the mountains to educate and organize the struggling campesinos that had suffered the most under Batista's rule and under all the previous regimes that neglected them. These were the same campesinos that supported Castro in the eastern mountain range where he was with his rebels. We were invited also to evangelize those campesinos that, in the remote areas of the mountains, had not had any real access to Christian ideas for many years.

My best friend Humberto and I decided to join them for a Holy Week vacation as we were both working in his father's electrical engineer company. On the way to the eastern mountain range to join these volunteers, we suffered a terrible car accident that killed Humberto and left me for many weeks recovering in a hospital, and many months more in a wheel chair. The doctors told my mother I would never walk again. My father, who had been sick with arteriosclerosis, died a few months later. I stood up with crutches for the first time for my father's funeral.

This accident changed my life. I was only nineteen years old. When they rescued me from the destroyed car somebody said "This one seems to be still alive." I came to remember that comment, vaguely, many months later as my memory had been blocked for some time when I lost consciousness.

The death of Humberto made a deep impact in my life. He was only twenty five years old, but was already very talented and well respected as a student leader who was actively involved in the university life and politics with a real potential to become a future great national figure. Additionally, he was also a leader in our Catholic organization, a man of deep faith and religious principles. He helped me encounter God in many ways. He taught me the gospels and the attitude Christ came to give us. He taught me to be a real patriot and love Cuba to the point of being ready to give my life for my country.

After the accident, I was bed ridden, and not able to move. Because of my lesions, I was not even allowed to read. I was left to reflect and cry. I was angry, and even complained to God for leaving me alive, young, inexperienced, and insecure. Instead, He took away my promising and successful friend. Nevertheless, I got up again, with a new sense of responsibility. For some reason, I was still alive. I was able to walk again and I promised never to deny anything God would ask me to do.

With a sense of a new beginning in Cuba, all my friends, who were actively involved in the new changes, exhorted me to join them and collaborate in the recovery of our country. I transferred from the Catholic private University where I was studying architecture, to the public three century old, prestigious Universidad de la Habana. This was recently reestablished after the revolution as it had been closed by Batista for the subversive activities of its students. I registered in the School of Social and Political Sciences. With the help of my friends and a walker I was able to move again. We all got involved in University politics, in the good sense. We edited well known activist student newspapers that had been suppressed by Batista's, and began to work on a new consciousness in the student population. All of us wanted to build up a new Cuba, finally based in Christian ideals with justice and peace for all. And we became very active in the student movements and university politics.

When the first elections took place for the student government, we won twenty seven places out of forty three delegations. The students trusted us for many reasons. We were clean and fresh and the student body seemed to be tired of sterile fights among political factions. We represented the ideals of many who had died against Batista. Also, there was the fear of the communists, who had never shown a clear opposition to Batista's regime. In fact, the communist party had supported Batista in many instances. Now, the communists again were trying to gain positions everywhere, including the student government of the Universidad de la Habana. The university had a long tradition of being the school for national politics. Castro made his first political "achievements" there, years before he went into the national scene.

Our first task as student leaders was to help create a deeper consciousness through our student newspapers. They appointed me editor of "Manicato" a university newspaper named after a "taino" Indian (original Cuban natives) battle cry. Manicato had a long tradition of defending the rights and the conscience of the university students and, of course, was silenced by Batista years before. Through Manicato and "Trinchera" another student newspaper, edited by my friends in the School of Law, we wanted to help the students build a new hope in this new beginning. The newspapers became very popular. So popular, that some non democratic forces infiltrating the government began to criticize us publicly. However, we proclaimed spirit that could build up a new Cuba after Batista's repressive regime.

Our freedom and euphoria were short lived as Castro fooled us all. At first, with his obvious ability to communicate to the masses, he persuaded everybody of his "good" intentions. Nevertheless, very soon he began ignoring the other democratic groups and giving progressively more importance and participation to the communist groups whose collaboration in the revolution against Batista was even questionable. A few months later, Castro's Revolution finally declared itself Communist. Then, persecution began to all who were not one hundred per cent in favor of that new forced turn of the revolution. Many groups, especially university student groups, protested and demonstrated.

The most significant protest happened against the visit of the Vice Premier of the Soviet Union to Havana. Anastas Mikoyan was guilty of sending the tanks against the 1956 student revolt in Hungary. We considered it an insult to have him place a wreath with the hammer and the sickle by the monument of José Martí, our Cuban patriot of the independence. Hundreds of students paraded to the Parque Central square a few minutes later and destroyed the wreath, with their reward being pelted by bullets from the government police or taken to jail.

All the newspapers gave overwhelming coverage, but almost at the same time, Castro confiscated all the democratic journals, and censored all TV and radio stations, including the ones with a very incorrupt and patriotic stand that were suppressed by Batista for opposing his regime. Castro used a very familiar tactic from other communist countries. He sent the "workers" militia to take over those sources of information with the excuse that it was necessary to "protect" the revolution. Soon, the government totally controlled, and took over all communications establishments.

Now, after the public protest that was openly against the communist regime, we students were constantly harassed by the paramilitary forces which fanatically defended the revolution. I was personally assaulted and beaten by these organized forces that Castro had infiltrated into the university. Castro called them the people's militia, the true defenders of freedom against the United States.

All over the country, but mostly in the University of Havana, student protesters, and young non-communists leaders were accused of being counter revolutionaries, terrorists, and spies for the United States government. Finally, in a big demonstration organized by Castro's forces in the main square of the university, three of us, Manuel Salvat, Alberto Muller, and me, were expelled from the university in an unprecedented and shameful action against freedom and human rights. Most university students present defended us and protected us from the mobs Castro had sent to attack us. It was May 1960. The government had taken over the Universidad de la Habana with his People's Militia, which was not even composed of university students, but by fanatic teen-agers organized by the repressive forces.

Then, back to the underground movement, the three leaders had to hide while continuing our now clandestine activities. As in the previous regime, the students began to organize themselves in groups and cells. The discontent against the communist regime was spreading over the whole country, especially through the student population who had no fear. But also the repression was being intensified through very sophisticated methods imported from the Soviet Union.

After a few months of working and organizing the underground, friendly sources in the government warned us of a new offensive against the student opposition leaders, primarily to eliminate once and for all, the "counter–revolutionary" student movement. The three of us who had been denounced publicly by all the newly controlled Press, were advised to leave the country. A few weeks later, we were leaving Cuba under Diplomatic Protection of the Brazilian ambassador. Our idea was to find international help outside Cuba.

We ended up in Miami, where many respectable revolutionary leaders were beginning to concentrate after escaping Cuba. They were organizing the resistance inside and outside Cuba. Our arrival in exile was highly publicized. Soon, the Central Intelligence Agency was contacting us and offering us help and weapons to return to Cuba. Reluctantly we accepted. We did not trust the C.I.A. maybe for all the bad press that gave the institution an air of mysterious international spying, but mainly, just gut feel. However, we needed help. We not only needed help against Castro's dictatorship, but now, openly, against the Soviet Union, who supported Castro, and Communist China, who supported Ernesto "Che" Guevara and Castro's brother Raul.

In the next months, Miami was the planning headquarters for overthrowing Castro. In Cuba, the underground kept growing stronger and the discontent with the regime was spreading all over the country. My two friends, Alberto and Manuel, infiltrated Cuba one after another, and all the student movements were united inside and outside Cuba.

The student movement was very powerful because we were conducting the most daring sabotage actions against the regime. The students severed many times the communications and electrical lines when Castro was giving his speeches. Electrical towers were toppled by using explosives. Leaflets and anti-Castro declarations appeared all around Havana in the most populous squares and boulevards. Many times these underground leaflets were thrown from high rise buildings into the busy streets. The idea was to inform the people of the situation as all the media had only the point of view of the government.

Every night, dozens of home made bombs exploded all around the cities annoying Castro's government to the point of exasperation and making them keep the security tighter and tighter around Castro and his puppet leaders. Nobody ever got killed from these bombs. They were in fact a ploy to tell the people that there was a strong opposition against Castro's regime. Again, we young students had no fear.

The opposition political organizations united under one front in Miami. I was assigned to stay in exile and to represent the student movement in the so called government of Cuba at War. I was the youngest member in a council composed by former presidents and illustrious politicians from democratic Cuba who were in exile. I felt very humbled and overwhelmed in the presence of such men who had survived many political crisis and persecution before against Batista. These were political figures who had even occupied elevated positions in government, even including Castro's government before he had declared himself a communist.

The invasion of The Bay of Pigs was supposed to liberate Cuba from the communist totalitarian regime and bring this new government to Cuba. José Miró Cardona was proclaimed as the new Cuban President at War after many days of exhaustive deliberations in Miami. When the group reached the decision we all went to New York for a historical Press conference to announce the government at war and the new President.

Miró Cardona, was a prominent lawyer who became famous during Batista's dictatorship. He had publicly accused Batista of his crimes and was forced to leave the country. After Batista was overthrown, Miró returned and Castro offered him the office of Prime Minister of the Republic. He occupied that important position until Castro began the infamous trials against Batista's supporters. Hundreds were sent to the firing squad after dubious and all too quick "legal" processes. Miró Cardona complained publicly, and after resigning from the government and being chastised by Castro, he had to go into exile, again.

After the Press conference, Miró Cardona came to me, the youngest member of the group, and asked me to accompany him to St. Patrick's Cathedral to pray. We had become friends during those meetings and have had long meaningful talks in which, of course, I just listened to the wisdom of that great man. On that day, he invited me alone, quietly away from the press, to kneel in that overpowering gothic cathedral to pray.

We were praying together for strength to carry the war to Cuba against communism and Castro, but also we shared the same fears about the future. Miró Cardona did not trust the C.I.A. either. He knew all too well that there were many international political schemes on the table and Cuba was just merely a gambling chip.

Years later, José Miró Cardona found out I was going to be ordained as a Catholic priest and attended my ordination for priesthood and sat in the first row of the Church. At the end of the eucharistic celebration, when I gave him the blessing as a priest, he hugged me, and crying profusely, he reminded me of our prayer in St. Patrick's Cathedral.

A few days after our proclamation of War in New York, and being called by the student underground movement in Cuba, I entered through the Havana shores in a small boat in a daring mission for the risk that implied by the underground reception team. This happened just 15 days before the Bays of Pigs invasion. Just before boarding the boat, I had just had received the terrible news that my younger brother Tomas, only 18 years old, had just been caught "conspiring against the government" with two other students, and sent to prison. My mother and my older brother were also detained and interrogated for a week when I landed in Havana.

I arrived in Cuba and was very impressed by the strength and well organized underground movement. I was assigned to join the rebels precisely in the same mountains where Castro "fought" his revolution. The campesinos who were also disillusioned with the communist government, were now supportive of the new rebels. I was taken by some brave members of the underground to a meeting point about twelve hours from Havana by car. However, when we were close to the point at the foothills of the mountains, Castro's forces had caught the campesinos that were waiting to take us to the rebel camp. In haste, we had to return to Havana.

A few days later, the invasion of Bay of Pigs took place. The underground movement was unaware of either the date or the place. Our telegraph agents, even though they had been trained by the CIA, and supposed to be in daily contact with them, were never informed. The CIA was controlling all communications.

We, in the underground, watched hopelessly as the communist government tanks went rolling through the streets of Havana, not knowing what was happening. The tanks were sent to the Bay of Pigs, which we thought was the most absurd place to land an invasion. It looked to us that all was planned for failure.

For two months, I was hiding in many different places in Havana as I was caught in the mayhem that followed the frustrated invasion. I saw with horror, the defeat and massacre of so many people who were abandoned by the country that had promised to help restore democracy in our suffering country.

The day after the invasion, Castro, in retaliation, tried many political prisoners, among them, my brother and his two companions. One very close friend of mine, Rogelio, who happened to be the top coordinator of the resistance in Cuba, was also in the group. They were all sentenced to death in the firing squad. My brother Tomas was spared, but only because the communist judge, as we found out later, had been saved by a surgery my father performed on him when he was a child. He sentenced my brother to 30 years in prison.

Through all of this, I had been reflecting, meditating, and pondering on my faith, my ideals, and my life. Our group of friends was decimated by the new oppressive forces. The firing squad was the new "altar" of sacrifice. All of my friends who died in front of Castro's firing squad cried with a loud scream which electrified the many who heard them, "Viva Cristo Rey"! Long live Christ the King! From his prison cell, my brother recognized the cry from his two companions as they were shot. After that brave attitude of the condemned to death, all the prisoners were systematically gagged so they could not yell the "Viva Cristo Rey" cry that provoked cries of support from the hundreds of student prisoners remaining in their cells.

For those of us who were spared, whether in jail or outside hiding in the underground, that became our battle cry. We were so proud for being able to die for our country, for freedom, for God. It was a living proof of our faith against the repressive forces of an evil regime that had fooled us all and betrayed our true revolution. At the invasion of Bay of Pigs we also sadly realized, that we had also been betrayed by the country we thought had wanted to help us in the fight against communism.

My brother Tomas spent 19 years in prison. Most of those years, he spent in the infamous prison of Isla de Pinos. During the Cuban war for independence in 1985 the Spanish authorities had used this island as a concentration camp for the patriots who aided the warriors. Ironically that was the place where my grandparents and family were sent for that reason 60 years before.

Tomas was finally released after a negotiation by the Christian Democrat government of Venezuela in those days. These negotiations allowed me to visit Cuba twice in 1978. The Cuban communist government, despite two death sentences on my head, allowed my entrance in Cuba to negotiate my brother's release.

After almost twenty years away from Cuba, I was able to experience my country's reality from within. I must confess that I was resigned to accept that a socialist-communist regime had achieved the changes that Cuba needed and had become an organized and disciplined country. Maybe the revolution had brought some positive changes, democracy was never able to bring. Nevertheless, I found with disillusion, a stifling Marxist-Leninist dictatorship, manipulated by a tight bureaucracy provoking an institutionalized chaos strictly designed to please the dictator. I found a devastated country with a dehumanized mass of people being ruled like children through propagandistic campaigns. The local media was totally controlled by the government. Censorship made people completely unaware of the changes in the outside world.

On the other hand, the government successfully manipulated the international press outside Cuba by praising the so called "achievements" of the revolution, while the reality in the country was quite different. The economy was in ruins, even though the Soviet Union supported Cuba with millions of dollars. After the fall of the Soviet Union, Castro blamed the United States and their "embargo", even though the Cuban government kept receiving US goods through Panama and Canada. These goods never reached the Cuban population but were used to maintain the newly developed tourist industry.

The once marvelous city of Havana, compared to Paris for its architecture, high culture and artistic life, was also literally in ruins. Its population, bored, poorly dressed and hungry, lined up in front of government distribution centers waiting for food. Masses of people wandered idly through the streets. Many, with annoying disrespect, accosted foreign visitors offering drugs or prostitution. The youth, obviously against the system, would mock the repressive forces agents who inquisitively and constantly combed the streets of Havana. There was a hidden black market for foreign films and music that were strictly forbidden by the regime.

In contrast, visibly present, there existed a small dominant class that seemed to enjoy all the privileges of former rich, high middle, and middle class of the past. This was the new ruling class of the high authorities in the communist party. In public ceremonies they vaunted their good European last model cars, expensive suits, and jewelry – the signs of luxury that had been identified as decadent capitalism in the beginning of the revolution.

I visited Cuba again in 2002, invited by Cuban bishops. I was able to travel through the 800 mile long island. The same disappointment came again to me as I could corroborate my impressions of Havana more than 20 years before. I visited terribly poor slums in several other cities that the government refused to recognize. Their inhabitants jokingly referred themselves as "the invisible" when the government insisted to claim that there were not slums in the country. Statistics were always "produced" by the government. The masses of wandering people on the streets were referred as "unemployment: 3%." It seemed that the communist government was not in the least interested on the problems of the Cuban people, but only on the international image ironically so well organized, in contrast, with propaganda, espionage, and "special" agents disguised as "cultural," infiltrated all over the world.

But, let us go back again to the times of the frustrated invasion of Bay of Pigs on April 17, 1961.

After the failure of the invasion, the underground movement had to get rapidly reorganized. Many were in jail, others trying to escape. I was transferred from post to post hiding in different "security" houses and homes. We understood the real burden and risk it was for the underground organization to take care of someone as "burned" as I was. So we finally decided that I should escape Cuba once again and find out what was happening in the world outside in order to help Cuba. Of my other two friends, Alberto was in jail, well recognized and sure to be sent to the firing squad. Manuel, after being detained among the thousands of suspects caught in Havana right after the invasion, was released. He fooled them by hiding his identity from the government agents who did not recognize him. Eventually, Manuel and I met in an underground high security place after his spectacular rescue jumping over a high wall in a house surrounded by the communist militia.

I finally escaped through the US Guantanamo Base on the eastern part of Cuba. I was there for two months putting together in my mind and my heart all that had happened. The first day after I jumped the fence, I found a little chapel on the base and I prayed with great relief and peace in my soul. I went there everyday trying to understand and assimilate all what was happening. I was finally sent to Miami with a group of young underground fighters from different anticommunist organizations that had also escaped by jumping to the Base.

Back in Miami, I had to make new plans for the future. I definitely thought I was going to die when I went to Cuba the last time. Now, I was still alive and questioning my future. I got engaged to my long time girlfriend, but within a month of the engagement I was called once again by our student organization to be part of a very specialized group to infiltrate Cuba and to reinforce the underground movement. The operation was being supported by the CIA. Reluctantly and despite the mistrust I still felt for the CIA, I accepted the new challenge. From Cuba our friends were desperate asking for help For two months a group of twelve received a very intense military training and tried to land off the coast of Cuba like once before.

However, the operation failed. Due to lack of information against Castro's well organized spy system, the reception team in Cuba was ambushed, and some of them killed. Our group was never able to land. Juanin, another very good friend, who took me to the train in Havana a few months before on my way to Guantanamo Base, was killed in the operation. He was a brave and extraordinarily mature twenty-one year old student and who was even thinking of becoming a priest when our war was over.

After that failed operation, and with hearts, souls, and trust in ruin, most of my friends decided to get married and finish their university studies with no other alternative in sight. As with them, I was also contemplating marriage and trying to figure out the rest of my life. I was twenty three years old. The peer pressure was very strong as we were a very close group of friends.

I had to make an intense discernment. After all those years of dedication to a "cause" I had been intrigued by a hidden restlessness deep in my mind and heart. In trying to make sense of all this, I contacted my very good friend a Jesuit priest who had been my spiritual adviser for many years. We talked for hours one day. I argued with myself and him. I certainly felt I had a calling but on the other hand I was very much in love with my fiancée. One day, after struggling for many weeks, I decided to argue openly with God, without holding back any excuses.

My accident five years before and all the experiences I had been through in those years, suddenly came as an affirmation to respond to that mysterious calling I felt in my heart. The restless feeling I struggled with all those years and through all of those ordeals. After a long painful talk with my fiancée and a most difficult and painful decision, I decided to enter the Jesuits and become a priest. It was not an easy decision and my fiancée and I had to work together through much pain and agony for both of us. In a way, I felt as if I was breaking with my past, but deep down, I knew this decision just reinforced my past. It made a lot of sense to me as a continuation of the type of life I had been accustomed to live and one that I was called to live.

Remarkably, the moment I made my final decision, everything became clear like in a new light and a more open perspective. Everything in my past began to make sense. I felt liberated and strong. But first, I had to cut all the strings that held me in place. I had to let things settle things with my fiancée and my mother, who just arrived from Cuba. Additionally, I had to sever my involvement in the student political organization. Before fully committing to the Jesuits, I had to wait one year to enter into the novitiate. It was a particularly very good year of reflection and reaffirmation. I was ready physically, emotionally, spiritually, but most importantly, I was ready to commit myself with the same passion, fortitude, and conviction that I had for the Revolution.

At 24 years of age, I entered the Jesuit novitiate in Spain.

I felt a real inner liberation and peace as I never felt before. My decision after the accident brought me to this new dimension in my life that I had never been able to articulate before. I felt like I had jumped to the unknown and I received in return a solid conviction and reassurance that I never thought was possible in the kind of world I had lived.

My faith kept me alive through all those long years of both study and work, in the midst of substantial changes in the world and in the Catholic Church. I thoroughly enjoyed my Jesuit training, which included a well balanced combination of humanistic classical studies with the development of theology through the ages. This training never lost sight of the necessities of the world socially and politically. It reinforced my experience on people and their personal and psychological problems. I studied in many parts of the world: Spain, Dominican Republic, Venezuela, Canada, Rome, and the United States.

I was blessed to find professors and spiritual guides all along through my studies and career. Among these, Gilles Cusson, S.J., a well known theologian, one of the top names in Ignatian spirituality, professor at the Gregorian University, advisor of Fr. Arrupe, then General of the Jesuits, and director of Tertianship, the last stage of formation to become a full-fledge Jesuit, helped me articulate my faith and guided me through my graduate studies and doctoral thesis of which this book is a summary.

I made close friends of different cultures, ages, races, social classes, and even different religions.

I worked for twenty years with students at Creighton, a Jesuit University in Omaha Nebraska in the medical school. Partially overlapping with my work at Creighton, I have worked at the ILAC Center, for promotion of integral education and health, in rural remote areas of the Dominican Republic, for more than thirty years. I have been there full time now for ten years.

Through all these years, I have reflected on my somewhat unusual life that, I thought, made me different than others. In many ways that was true. However, I have found on my way many different characters and people from different backgrounds and histories who had come to the same conclusions of an attitude in life that I found. The questions that I have encountered throughout my life and the answers I have found seem to be, surprisingly, the same as theirs. This is one of the mysteries of life, each one of us is unique. However, we all shared something in common: we were together in this deal. We also seem to have a universal task or responsibility we must be aware of or discover. We all feel that mysterious calling, a challenge to learn, to discover, and to get truly and actively committed to life.

Even through my own mistakes, I have found that overwhelming inner force that is, definitely, greater than myself. However, this force is surprisingly personal and personable. It makes me the center of the world and, at the same time, an infinitesimal part of an intriguing universe beyond my reach. This force, inexplicably, has been constantly and consistently drawing me towards other beings like me, who seem to form a social universe in which all are different, but at the same time, basically the same, forming an interconnecting and dynamic net.

My personal discovery through my life, is the same discovery, as I said, many others through different circumstances have found through their own lives.

This inner liberating force, that I feel very deep inside, is definitely, though veiled, in every human being in the universe. It is awaiting discovery by each individual. I now understand that I should share with all others the particular and even peculiar way I discovered my own purpose of life and that inner force that, through my life, has been leading me all along toward happiness. There is certainly an innate quest for happiness in each one of us. I definitely need to share how I discovered my own way to happiness so that even in some small way, it may be able to help others to find theirs.

Ernesto Fernández-Travieso, S.J.

## PROLOGUE BY THE AUTHOR

In the Declaration of Independence of The United States of America, the Pursuit of Happiness appears as one of the "rights" a citizen should have in order to enjoy freedom as a full human being. Everybody agrees: we have the right to be happy! The pursuit of happiness is a human right that should include all the others. Maybe we don't pay too much attention to this "right" because the concept of happiness seems to be too abstract in our materialistic oriented world of today. Also, happiness is a very complicated concept to understand. So many people tend to explain happiness in easier superficial ways usually in economically or emotionally related terms.

On the other hand, when we speak about rights we usually overlook one very important fact. We like to speak about our rights, but seldom consider our duties. Our society today, proclaims the rights of the individual almost against its duties to society, as if the commonwealth of society would threaten the individual welfare. Possibly this has happened as a reaction to communism and even socialism that definitely have exaggerated the duties of the individual toward society. The obvious result has been the flagrant dehumanization of society and the loss of personal identity. What they have caused is an appalling destruction of the societies they originally intended to "rescue" from the "evil monster of capitalism."

It surprised me that after the collapse of the Soviet Union the world did not hear much about the true horrors of communism and its consequences. The crudest consequence was the way the individuals were absorbed, near annihilation, by the state, depriving them from their initiative and desire to work and to improve personally. Visiting today many of the countries that suffered under communism, we can see how these people barely survived by holding quietly to their dignity and their innate desire to claim their individual human rights. The communist paradise was proven a fallacy over and over.

However, it puzzled me to observe how the people in the "free world" did not hear enough how communism truly damaged those countries. Now that the system collapsed, the many truths could finally come out into the open. I wondered if this lack of publicity was intentional... Was it because the media did not want, for some reasons, to uncover the similarities between the communist world and the so called "capitalist democracies"?

Today, there still exist some countries under the bluntly archaic system of communism. The people there, controlled by the ruling "new class" ignore what is happening in the world. The media, controlled by the leaders in power, in those countries, is still trying to "brainwash" the masses.

But if we reflect on the way our "free world" media practically manipulates the masses, we might come to the realization that there are many similarities with the communist regimes. Some critical observers are alarmed by these "hidden persuaders," who seem to be attacking and destroying family values, spiritual beliefs, through insidious "campaigns" directed to disintegrate all what has been accomplished through centuries of growth. Some radical "worriers" wonder if today the human beings are able to grow freely and exercise their rights under the heavy pressure of the media, controlled by the economic powers. In a communist regime the enemy is one and only, easy recognizable as the government that imposes the rules. However in capitalism, the "enemy" cannot so easily be recognized, is all around where power and selfishness abides, beginning with our very own selves.

Happiness has to include both the individual and the society. Our rights and our duties have to keep that delicate balance that is not so easy to achieve: a continuous dichotomy and a constant struggle to balance the two.

One very important concept that seems endangered today in our societies is the real meaning of happiness. The media appears to insist in selling to us a definition of happiness that suppresses whatever idea that goes beyond easy pleasure and materialistic accomplishment. The youth is openly bombarded with ideas of equating happiness with "fun", casual sex, obsessive vanity, and as a consequence complete irresponsibility and instant gratification. Again, no talk about duties, and if they mention human rights, it seems as if the only possible "right" for the common fellow is to become a better consumer in a materialistic society.

Today we live in a "stress" that is killing us. We don't seem to have time for reflection and for silence of the heart. If we could find time to be away from the worldly over activity for a while, instead of letting us be carried away by the constant activity that only creates anguish and loneliness, we would become aware of what we human beings truly are. We could touch the profound reality that lies beneath and beyond our "active productive lives."

We humans are creative, producers and workers, in every sense, but it seems, in such a rat race, we live without knowing from where we come, or where we are going. We don't have time to think!

It struck me when I was very young, what I heard Gandhi said as he visited New York in those days for the first time. Observing the regular confusion of the people in the streets of New York, he asked the journalists who were interviewing him "And when do these people meditate"?

If, as we usually say, we are in the search for happiness, we must stop and think, we must reflect in whom we are, where we are going, what is the purpose of my life. Where are we going as a universal humanity?

This book is the result of my own search for happiness even though I never thought I was really searching for happiness. I was just "living" or furthermore, racing over hurdles through all my life.

Again, this book is the result of my many experiences through all my life searching, and in many ways, corroborating what has been my faith all along through good times and bad. This faith, I have received through many friends and incredible individuals. All of them have left an impression and imprinted indelible marks in the person I am still developing to be.

This book leads to a search for that happiness all of us yearn, but most of the time we miss, because we are looking for it in the wrong direction. Maybe we expect happiness to be a destination, while we should most assuredly look for it in the journey itself.

We will search through history in the growth and mainly in the developing of Western thought through the centuries. We have certainly found answers through experience and reflection. We will go from the Babylonians, whose advanced culture and technology evolved the world from the pre-history into new unsuspected dimensions. We will revisit the Greek culture whose philosophy found new levels of thinking. Then, we will study the Jewish tradition that endowed history with a positive vision of life that still surprises us in the world today. Finally, the Romans contributed a universal idea to all humanity from the ancient civilizations to the modern world.

However, we will go deeper in that evolutionary process of human thinking trying to find a purpose of life that transcends life itself. We will talk about a consciousness that would go beyond cultures, races and religions.

This book is not an exhaustive academic treaty. It is rather an invitation to read more, and most of all, to reflect about our own individual experiences in life in the light of the experiences and reflections of humanity through the ages.

Today many questioning searchers look into the orient in order to find answers. Certainly the Western world has lost to the incredibly profound philosophy of the Eastern world. We have lost the inner values of reflection and meditation into higher human dimensions. Our world of technology has made us lose this transcendental dimension.

Thomas Merton, a great mystic of our times, died in the orient, ironically electrocuted by a defective General Electric fan. Merton was searching for a more profound reality in order to incorporate it into his own spiritual experience. There are also "prophets" today who continue to make us think and reflect on the values of life and a true direction toward happiness. Mother Theresa of Calcutta, challenging these times of obsessive vanity, pleasure, and money, died spent and wrinkled, but intriguingly and paradoxically happy, giving love to the outcast, the marginal, and the forgotten. The signs are there!

In this world, apparently ruled by a darkness that includes violence, materialism, lack of conscience, superficiality, and waste, there is still hope. It seems, though, that human beings can still choose for light against darkness. Furthermore, they can become light themselves to dispel darkness. For those who choose positive light there will be a different world. We are on a new century, on a new millennium!

Let us wake up from our lethargy and despair and search for a way towards true happiness. We might find out that, as we said before, the way to happiness lays on the search itself!

# PART I

# THE PROBLEM WITH HAPPINESS

## INTRODUCTION

What does it mean to be happy and fulfilled? Everybody looks for happiness. We yearn for it all through our lives, and yet most people generally fail to find it. That is why happiness is definitely a problem. Happiness is always a challenge.

One of the few things that all people have in common is the desire to be happy. We are born with this desire even though we may not always be aware of it. As we mature, through reason and reflection, we become aware of the true importance of this overriding desire that can draw us to the transcendental level of human life.

We all have moments in which we can say we have experience happiness. These sparks of emotional intensity inspire us to keep looking, searching, and hoping for something as elusive as happiness.

Thousands of volumes have been written about the happiness we so often talk about. Nevertheless, despite our best efforts we are seldom able to articulate exactly what happiness is.

Our consumer society panders to our desire for happiness. Our mass media is witnessing our failure to find it. Youth become an easy prey to the consumer society that exploits their innate desire offering all sorts of endless surrogates. All these escapist vices like drugs, alcohol, hedonistic obsession of beauty, animal sexual pleasure in which love is not included, cater to personal and egotistical self-indulgence. These means for quick easy happiness are sold today in the streets promising true happiness. Fortunately, intelligent, thinking and reflective young person cans recognize the cruel manipulation to which they are objects. Happiness must be a far more serious and profound reality.

Nick Vujicic, is a young man of 21 from Australia who was born with no arms and no legs. After his painful struggles to accept his condition, that included contemplating suicide, he has now completed university studies. Nick has now become a motivational speaker who finds great fulfillment in going all across the globe sharing his story of courage with thousands of young people.

The history of both East and Western cultures provides us with multitudes of scrolls and pages on centuries of reflection on these fundamental questions and the search for answers. Many questions have been left unanswered. Some people give up the quest. Maybe the weak of heart, the superficial hedonists cannot make the steep climb. Others succumb through fear, never able to free themselves from that powerful enemy that can keep us immature for the rest of our lives. However, most keep going, moved by that inner desire for happiness at the heart of human life.

If we just stop and reflect –something so difficult in our present busy lives– about the centuries of these writings and thoughts. We may find a way and a direction that could really make sense. Maybe we could avoid sterile and frustrating efforts in looking for happiness in the wrong places.

Of course, we know this search for true happiness will take great effort and tenacity. If we decide to commit ourselves to the pursuit of happiness, life would definitely turn into a fascinating adventure full of unimaginable pleasant surprises. Many have done this. Most have found this quest to be the unique force to lead us through life.

Plato would equate happiness with wisdom and knowledge. Its pursuit would take us to immortality. How many today would really think of "knowledge" and "wisdom" when referring to "happiness"? How many would just stay in the level of materialistic or economic achievement? How many never experience more than merely sensual or material pleasure?

It seems absurd to define happiness in such narrow terms. On the other hand, if we ask every human being for a definition of happiness, we would get discouraged right away. Each person would offer us a different answer. Even though we suspect there must be a common definition that should satisfy us all, perhaps the best strategy would be if we reverse our approach. It would be easier to agree in a negative definition: what happiness is not.

## 1) WHAT HAPPINESS IS NOT

A happiness that does not include all the aspects and levels of the human person can never be real happiness. We are born to be unique and individual. Soon enough, we learn that we are also social beings. We need one another, and not only in the utilitarian sense, as Rousseau maintained in his "Emile", but also spiritually and sentimentally. Furthermore, we seem to know that besides the personal and social levels we move to a third level of existence. We grow beyond our own limitations into a spiritual and universal dimension that would lead us towards transcendence.

Indeed, our personal relationships are truly important in our lives. We need family, friends, support groups, communities, in order to function "normally" in our daily lives. However, our social being, cannot be satisfied only by being just part of a "group." We humans seem to have a desire to go beyond our limits. At that point, our individual and social dimensions join together in quest leading us to transcendence by embracing the whole infinite universe that surrounds us. In spite of our own limitations there exists something "cosmic" within us. This sort of spiritual instinct calls us to transcend beyond our own reach. There is also a feeling of social responsibility in us that alls us to develop and to be actively "useful" to the whole world and universe. This sort of "spiritual instinct" will lead us beyond our reach, not making us irresponsible escapists, but truly committed and involved human beings.

Our deduction is that we cannot find true happiness unless we take in consideration these three levels or dimensions of human experience: the psychologically personal, the social, and the spiritually universal. We could never be happy unless we follow this transcendental calling we feel inside. This calling must be realized in a social context with the almost unlimited possibilities the world, the universe, is offering us today.

In the particular social, political, and economic systems the world is offering us today, can we find happiness? A system that ignores the individuals by reducing them to mere numbers in the social conglomerate, as communism, socialism, under different disguises, keep proclaiming cannot certainly offered a kind of happiness "designed" by the state. Doubtless, not even the dictators, who present themselves as "redeemers" of the oppressed, are able to enjoy any kind of happiness themselves. These who foolishly consider power, eventually end up consumed by misery and lonely emptiness.

On the opposite extreme, a system that separates the individuals from each other making them selfish and materialistic consumers, cannot lead towards true happiness either. Capitalism proposes false hopes through self-seeking pleasures and material achievements as ends for life. Reality proves today that irresponsible competition is bringing more social and economical differences and injustices. These increasing differences are appearing not only between social classes, but also between rich and poor countries to the point of destruction of entire societies.

Both answers seem completely dehumanizing and are promoting societies of slaves.

A happiness that reduces us to a purely animal or mechanical level of experience cannot be true happiness. Happiness can never be obtained under dehumanizing conditions, regardless how well our basic needs are satisfied, even if they are ever satisfied. Both of these extremes have proven in history to deny our basic desire for happiness by blocking our personal and transcendental developing process. Of course, the ruling classes in both systems enjoy levels of entertainment and luxuries that go beyond imagination. These successful rich and famous celebrities are almost imposed by the media today as models or "idols". Their lifestyle and excesses are scandal to the poor of the world.

Curiously, all that publicity cannot hide the misery and loneliness of those who claim to have found happiness "world" style. These live in guild cages, unaware of the masses outside. Worst of all, these masses, manipulated by the media, seem to be falling into the same trap. They keep feverishly pursuing riches following a self-destructive dream.

No wonder there are so many people today that choose to escape reality in vices, drugs, alcohol, irresponsible sex and frivolity, that seem to assure them immediate "happiness". The world is practically in chaos today: war, injustice, moral depravity, hunger and poverty in ones, opulence and waste in others, corruption of power, and the guilty ignorance of these conditions by the most. This reality provokes lack of interest, apathy and cynicism even in those who could be doing something to alleviate this critical condition in some way.

Escapism and apathy are traps. These worsen our anguish and insecurity, and only lead us to the internal and external destruction of our persons and our society.

Those who have not yet fallen into this dehumanizing trap, must awaken to the cry of humanity. We must certainly take action and try to embark in a true adventure to find happiness in life for our own sakes and that of everyone else.

*Before we begin our search, let us consider a previous necessary step. Let us define more specifically what we truly know about ourselves as human beings, what we really are, our purpose in life, and the end for which we seem to exist. Let us revise, in the light of contemporary authors what the human being has found through years of experience, study, and reflection. Please, follow me in what I have learned from others about the purpose of life and what I have found in my own life through experience.*

## 2) THE PURPOSE OF LIFE

We cannot begin our search for happiness unless we can find if there is a purpose to life. For centuries philosophers have overwhelmed us with different ideas, sometimes contradictory, about the purpose of human life and the reasons we have for existing both as an individual and a social being. There are some who have denied there is any purpose to life. Others have a very bleak and fatalistic view of life in general. However, most thinkers, especially those who have contributed to the development of the Western civilization, recognize a positive purpose to life. In recent centuries, the human sciences, especially psychology and sociology, have shed new light on that positive vision of life both individually and universally.

Victor Frankl survives the horrid concentration camp by finding a positive meaning for life. Yes, life is worth living, regardless the trials and suffering we must go through.

Carl Jung, Sigmund Freud's contemporary, goes way beyond his popular colleague, so caught up in his sexual obsessions. Jung defines human life in a higher dimension than what Freud was ever able to study. Jung defines life as a process of transcendence from nature to consciousness. Human beings, while growing in consciousness, want to go beyond what the limitations natural instincts have imposed on them. They try to free themselves and go beyond these instincts in a process of personal transformation towards an infinite supernatural spiritualization. The human beings grow from natural into supernatural spiritual beings. There is indeed a positive and transcendental purpose to life even beyond our human dimension.

Even Nietzsche, as negative as he usually is, cannot deny the positive purpose of life the human being possesses. In his Zarathustra, Nietzsche explains how the human being must turn himself into a "creator" through life in order to become fully human. He will suffer loneliness, his most dreadful enemy, but he must never lose his courage. Humans would go through life, which sometimes appears as a desert, transforming themselves always into higher stages of an evolving life.

Most seem to agree that human beings develop through an intricate dynamic process. Some author refers to this growing in consciousness as "conscientization" which takes the individual to a transcendence that seems to be mysteriously planted inside every human being as a kind of spiritual instinct. The human being thinks and knows that he thinks. In this we recognize our differences with animals. They think, there is no doubt about it, but they are not aware of it. Knowing that they think, the human beings are able to reflect, to reason, to and to learn. We humans learn while living through positive achievements and also our shameful errors and mistakes. Through this learning process, we individuals definitely are able to transcend beyond our own instincts and limitations. Wisdom and Knowledge, as Plato explains, are universal forces in all human beings and lead them to happiness.

If we want to understand our purpose of life, according to thinkers and philosophers, we cannot encounter it as a static concept. They all seem to agree that life is truly a dynamic process of personal and social evolution. Thus, the purpose of life can only be understood in the context of this dynamic process of "conscientization". By following him as he grows, discover, learns, and understands himself and others, his world, his universe, his purpose of life will surely be unfolding through his different stages in life.

This process will be developing in each individual along his life through the different stages of growing and learning. From his almost instinctively childhood, into a growing in wisdom mature adulthood, the human being evolves towards new and higher dimensions.

Pierre Teilhard de Chardin, S.J., helps us immensely in the understanding of our own process of growing in consciousness and wisdom: a process of personalization.

---

*Finding Teilhard's readings as a student marked a personal turning point in my life. His own fascinating history, his writings from the front in the First World War, his life as a paleontologist when his group discovered the Peking Man, his persecution when his writings about Evolution, in those days, opposed the views of the Vatican, and was forbidden to publish and speak in public. Some years after his death, which happened in New York on Easter Sunday 1956, Teilhard was accepted and increasingly recognized as the theologian who reconciled Science and the Christian Faith. His writings, rich in mysticism, filled our lives as young Jesuits and strengthen my faith with new hopes into the future. Reading Teilhard, my horizons were opened into new perspectives. I felt as if my life and my vocation expanded to universal dimensions. I must share Teilhard's most important vision of life and its purpose through the stages of life, the way that I was personally experiencing.*

## 3) A HUMANIZING PROCESS THROUGH LIFE

Pierre Teilhard de Chardin, a French Jesuit, enlightens the path to find happiness through the process of becoming a "person." He explains how human beings become increasingly conscious through the different stages of life. He calls this process: *"hominization"*. In this world apparently so dehumanized, Teilhard's reflections can definitely bring us a breath of fresh air into our quest for happiness.

Teilhard states simply and boldly, what the purpose of life for the human being is: *to find and obtain happiness*. Right there we encounter a statement that can lead us to encouraging personal answers. Teilhard declares that happiness cannot be found "the animal way" just by satisfying our animal appetites and instincts. Happiness, in the human being involves a more intricate design of elements to fulfill his needs and desires. His human fulfillment must consider the three levels of human existence: the personal, the social, and the universal. Man lives in a process of evolution in which he is becoming more aware of himself, others, and the universe. By virtue of his *hominization*, says Teilhard, man has become a reflective and critical living being; and his gift of reflection brings with it two other formidable properties, the power to perceive what may be possible, and the power to foresee the future.

Teilhard's hominization theory brings us to unlimited heights, ending in a true spiritualization, that is, in a supernatural transcendence that includes the whole universe. It is a universal movement towards the future that intimately includes the personal and the social. In other words, the individual growing in consciousness fully becomes a person while joining an evolutionary movement that ends in God, the supreme consciousness of all that universal movement.

Consciousness, therefore according to Teilhard, is the purpose of life and the purpose of the entire universe. There seems to be only one direction for Man to seek happiness, a mainstream of life. Teilhard invites us to join willingly to climb towards a fuller dimension of freedom, of sensibility, or inner vision.

This personal movement will happen through the different stages of life that lead the particular individual and all human beings to find true happiness. Teilhard calls these three stages: "Centration," "Decentration," and "Super-centration."

If Man is to be fully himself and fully living, he must, 1) be centered upon himself; 2) be "de-centered" upon "the other", 3) be super-centered upon a being greater than himself.

**Centration**

Teilhard declares that Man is Man only if he cultivates himself, not only physically, but also intellectually and morally. The human being must get to know himself, work constantly on himself to introduce more order and more unity on his ideas, his feelings, and his behavior. This first phase is defined as the "making and finding one's own self. The human being in his *self-identification* stage discovers an acceptance of himself, his positives as well as his negatives, be realistically aware of his potentialities. Centration, self-identification or self acceptance, seems to be a necessary step in order to keep growing in the personalization process. Centration could correspond to childhood, according to a chronological view. Certainly the early years of a human being's life are usually identified with this stage. Nevertheless, in practice, this stage may last all of one's life. The human being is basically a growing child trying to understand himself, the others, and the universe. As a child, naturally selfish, the human being seems to have the task of growing less egotistical when he reaches the next levels of maturity.

**De-centration**

It follows Centration as a necessary condition to growth in life. Nevertheless, De-centration seems to be a necessity in order to experience self-identification, Centration and de-centration evolve dialectically.

It could be defined as union of one's being with other beings who are his equals. After accepting oneself, the human being is ready to accept and to love others. We cannot reach our ultimate without emerging from ourselves by uniting ourselves with others in such a way as to develop through this union an added measure of consciousness. At this stage the human being discovers real love, which in its fullest meaning implies de-centration, self donation, and even self sacrifice for others. Paradoxically the human being will become more fulfilled the more he gives himself to others. Love, in all its forms, drives the human being to associate his individual center with other centers.

In our early adolescence we begin to find others, need others, and enjoy the company of others. We like to be accepted by others, even to be admired by others. We discover teamwork and how to work with others. Maybe our relationships tend to be "economical", in the sense that we like to give in order to receive, to experience gratification. As we grow we experience the true meaning of De-centration.

This is the time in life to discover friendships and to fall in love. But De-centration, also as a concurrent dialectical force with Centration would move the individual through all his life, making him always more understanding, more conscious.

We must react, declares Teilhard, against the selfishness which causes us either to close in on ourselves, or to force our domination upon others, there is a way of loving – bad sterile way – in which we try to possess rather than give ourselves. Self-giving love, the love of self-donation, is the only love that completes and fulfills the person.

## Super-centration

The third step in life's upward progress is Super–centration. The dialectical process between Centration and De-centration leads the individual to this new step in consciousness.

Waiting for us, is a center of higher order. We must, then, do more then develop our own selves –more than give ourselves to another who is our equal– we must surrender and attach our lives to one who is greater than ourselves. Self donation in love finds now a greater object than ever before: *something or someone that includes everything else*. The new center of our lives must be indeed a unifying cause that respects our individuality, but also takes us to higher and universal dimensions. Teilhard identifies this supreme center with God. He affirms that our personal and universal process of consciousness and personalization will take us to God himself.

On reaching adulthood, the human being has supposedly grown over his self-identification by accepting himself. He has found and accepted others and his own place in society.

He is capable of understanding life and his purpose of life with some wisdom and experience. Mature and responsible, the super-centered human being gets involved, not looking precisely for approval or reward. He moves now in a new dimension of freedom and fulfillment. He acts upon life doing what is right, that what gives him inner satisfaction, and peace of mind. This fulfillment can never be confused with passing superficial joy.

Super-centration implies the highest understanding of love: self-donation to the universe, to mankind, or to God who includes them all.

Teilhard seems to keep relating Man's purpose in life to the pursuit of happiness through life. True happiness is happiness of growth on each stage of life.

## Love and compassion

According to Teilhard, the human being is the most developed (or progressed) form of consciousness in universal evolution. Through love he would obtain a higher sensibility, freedom, and inner vision. Love is, therefore, the direction of evolution. Love leads to union and happiness in a higher dimension of reality. By evolving from nature to consciousness, the universe discovers love as the cohesive element that will eventually produce harmony in the plurality among the individuals on earth.

Love has moved the history of humanity in mysterious ways. Just studying the Renaissance times that shaped up our western civilization, we find outstanding scientists, artists, discoverers, creative geniuses, and saints, who left a mark in history. They sacrifice themselves and endure all sorts of persecution for the sake of humanity. In times of universal crisis, great saints denied themselves to help others to restore new hope in humanity. Francis of Assisi, Ignatius of Loyola, Phillip of Neri, Theresa of Avila and John of the Cross showed us what the Gospel attitude truly was in moments of confusion. Some even suffered persecution by the same Church they were saving.

Mozart, Beethoven, Bach, and Handel left us the most beautiful music ever composed. They transcended all human possibilities.

In our times, scientists like the Curies, personal friends of Teilhard, even though they were confessed agnostic, gave their lives, literally, to humanity.

All of these great heroes in history, like many others, lived through Super-centration. They found something or someone greater than themselves to live for. Their lives give us courage to follow our quest for life and the pursuit of happiness.

Unfortunately, there are also many bad examples of selfish geniuses through history who have destroyed complete nations with their evil maniacal obsession for power.

Love is, therefore, the direction of personal, social, and universal evolution. Even though love cannot be measured, a spiritual force such as it is, its effects can certainly be perceived in the personal level. Love shows its effects in *compassion*. Compassion means to feel with, to identify with others, especially in their suffering and struggles.

Compassion is a sign of progress in the way of consciousness. Compassion is the effect of true love. The truly compassionate person is sensitive and humble. He is lovingly present to the ones in need. This sensitivity is usually the synthesis of self-knowledge and experience. He is humble because he is aware of his own weaknesses and limitations. The compassionate person accepts himself and knows he needs others too. He feels one with "the others," once giving, other times receiving.

The compassionate person is the one who seems to understand the three levels of love. The three loves must grow from one to the next step: love of oneself (Centration), love of "the others" (Decentration), and love of the universe (Super-centration).

Compassion, as it is based on love, implies a deep understanding of *justice*. There is no love unless justice, its practical application, is sought first. It seems that justice must come first as the basic attitude, and love begins only after justice has been fulfilled. Justice, therefore, appears as a consequence of love and compassion.

*Pierre Teilhard de Chardin has shown us a way, a process of life that leads to happiness. Nevertheless, it seems we have taken a leap into the future without following the proper steps to reach these conclusions. It would help us, at this point, to back up in history and find how this train of thought developed through the ages. Then, Teilhard's view of evolution and the future can be followed as it develops through the history of humanity. Let us reviewed how the ancient civilizations confronted the fundamental questions of life. Their answers can definitely teach us a personal way to pursuit happiness.*

## 4) THE SEARCH FOR HAPPINESS IN ANCIENT CIVILIZATIONS

The history of ancient civilizations can be of remarkable value for us in our search for happiness. The ancients began to write history when they felt compelled to care about themselves and their life among others in the world. They deal with the fundamental questions of life. They question everything around them, including themselves. Either the ancient cultures are built and developed around the answers the human beings find; or perhaps the other way around, after years of struggling they come up with some answers as a product of their cultures.

Since the birth of civilization we have been trying to answer the same questions of life. As soon as we became a thinking being, we faced the same question: is there a purpose to life? If so, what is it?

We can study how humans have dealt with their own personal mysteries of life, in their social awareness, and in their ways of interpreting the universe.

Most great ancient civilizations have presented a bleak vision of the human life and the universe with no clear purpose in life. This negativity must respond to their constant struggle against nature and against each other. We are vulnerable to the attack of most anything surrounding us, even the gods who seem to use and abuse us arbitrarily.

Even though this fatalistic and pessimistic view of life pervades most ancient civilizations, they find answers that confirm at least these two points: the desire to live, and the desire for transcendence. These answers are merely ideal fantasies to escape from what it seems to be man's terrible fate. Suffering and death affirm the absurdity of human life.

Still, the testimony of this search for a purpose to life keeps appearing through history. The questions are written on cave walls in pre-historic drawings, and are raised to the sky in the awesome Egyptian pyramids. There seem to be answers in the mysterious smiles of the Korés and the sophisticated art of the Greeks. Our desire to live, despite suffering and struggle, is an historic fact. Our desire to transcend, to go beyond our own physical and natural limitations, against all odds, is also proven by our anguish expressed in the history of literature and art to this day.

*Let us choose, from the ancient civilizations, those that contributed the most to the Western thinking. Among them, are the Greek, whose culture directly influenced the Roman Empire, the cradle of our Western culture. We must study the Sumerian-Babylonians who contributed writing, with which humans were able to communicate, in the beginning of civilization in history. Let also reflect on the Jewish culture that gave the world a new spiritual and universal vision of life.*

*Even though we cannot overlook the rich ancient oriental cultures, we must concentrate in these three cultures. These cultures have contributed the most extensive literary documents to the history of the Western World. They have also contributed the most important sources to today's universal thinking.*

## 5) THE GREEKS

*Human beings against arbitrary gods.*

At the age of enlightment in Greece, Aristotle and Plato philosophize with the aristocracy about the question of life's purpose. Aeschylus and Sophocles offer cathartic relief for people through their tragic plays. Euripides goes further. He brings tragedy with its philosophical questions to the common person of the new democracy which is beginning to rise in Greece. His answers generally come from above ("deus ex machina") with no possibility for further discussion.

Nevertheless, the Greeks always manage to keep the questions alive in the human being, down to earth, mixed with their daily domestic "tragedies". In the tragedies of Euripides, especially, the myths are mixed with the commonest problems of the middle class life, as in Medea, for example, and her domestic drama. The Greeks openly challenged the design of the gods to the limit. The myths appear terribly human in the eyes of the Greek people who dare to invest their gods with human passions.

Greek culture contributes to our search for the purpose to life with deep insights. Wisdom and knowledge are the main virtues sought by the Greeks. At the peak of their culture they deal with the questions of life with a lot more philosophy and wit than many of the other ancient cultures. They seem to find a way to cope with the cruelty of existence so vividly portrayed in their tragedies. Their starting point is that man lives in constant insecurity. No one escapes insecurity. The gods will punish humans for the least mistake and fault. (hamartia) The play *Oedipus,* by Sophocles is a good example of a play about man's radical insecurity. Oedipus is exceptionally intelligent, a fact proven when he guesses the Sphinx's riddle about the human condition. Oedipus is the noblest of men, but he falls suddenly and unexpectedly into utter misery and destruction.

Through all Greek mythology we observe how the human beings always try to cope with the design of the gods and the forces of nature. Prometheus steals the fire from Vulcan to give it back to the mortals on earth, a precious acquisition for humanity. Prometheus, however, is tortured most horribly for his audacity as if he had committed a crime. Electra is "used" by the gods to do justice for the assassination of her father Agamennon. Her god-inflicted obsession to kill her mother Clytemnestra, makes her a tragic slave of passion and revenge.

The Greeks develop a philosophy of life in order to survive the tragedies of life. This philosophy is chanted by the chorus in the theatre as if to educate the people in wisdom. The Greeks go much further than anyone else in their conclusion of how to face life. They must find a cathartic relief in fraternal solidarity. This solidarity in the tragic absolute is symbolically expressed in the Greek theatre where the people in the audience are invited not only to sympathize but also to share the suffering with the heroes as they are confronting their irrevocable fate. Through fraternity and solidarity in facing the tragic human condition, the Greeks become more aware of the attitude they must develop as they face the gods and life.

Apart from acoustical purposes, the theatre seems to have been designed to promote solidarity of all humanity in mind. The spectators form a living embrace with the characters on stage, and the chorus becomes a link between the audience and the actors. The chorus, in the orchestra, reflects what is happening on stage and stirs compassion for the characters in the tragedy. At times the chorus gives practical advice both to the characters and to the spectators. The essential principle of this advice is to use wisdom to educate themselves in order to learn how not to force their chances, how not to irritate their gods, how not to trespass their limits. Otherwise, as in the tragedies and myths, the wrath of the gods is unbounded, slashing not only the arrogant guilty who dares to challenge them but also the innocent. Humans are always the losers and the victims; both nature and the gods seem to be against them at one point or another.

## 6) THE BABYLONIANS

*Human beings as victims of the gods.*

Long before the Greek, the Babylonians have already been dealing with the myths in literary form for several centuries. In the time period, just before written language was invented, declares Thomas Cahill, the Sumerians, from which the Babylonians descended, experienced a cultural explosion. This was comparable to the technological revolution in our XIX and XX Centuries A.D. In this ancient historical period there was a radical expansion of the agricultural communities around the vast green territories defined by the rivers Tigris and Euphrates. This flourishing was caused by the innovative use of agriculture and the movement of cattle and sheep which enabled the development of transportation by land and sea. The wheel was invented with almost unlimited possibilities for ground transportation. Sailing ships navigated rivers and seas.

The oven constituted a major step in the process of civilization. It made possible the use of metals and pottery. Baked clay brought life to the tablets that would be used for writing and eventually, for literature.

Sumerians were the first to elaborate new techniques for building beyond simple housing. Monumental sculpture and architecture in stone appeared for the first time in history. Decorative relief, the mold to make bricks, the arch, the vault, and the dome, were among the elements that created a new dimension in history. These new developments stimulated commercial and business transactions that required great concentrations of people, possessions, and riches. Cities were formed. Huge storage space was needed for commercial products which needed inventories to be recorded. These commercial records in clay tablets finally gave rise to writing.

When the first word was ever written in a small clay tablet, Sumerians were capable of dominating the Mesopotamian territories. In these cities were signed commercial agreements and truces, and occasional political treaties that extended as far as the valley of the Nile in North Africa, to the valley of the Indus in the Far East.

Thanks to archeology, we have been able to record the high degree of sophistication achieved by the Sumerians in the twenty five city-states they founded along the Tigris and the Euphrates. One of them was Babylon. In these cities were developed mathematics and medicine. From there they wrote their myths and developed their religious beliefs.

Gilgamesh stories are popular among the Sumerians in the third millennium B.C. Hundreds of years later Babylonian scribes (ca. 1750, XVIII century B.C.) repeat and revise these stories that eventually become the epic poem *Gilgamesh*, preserved and found in Assurbanipal's library. The poem expresses the adventurous drive of man (Gilgamesh) and his tragic search for an immortality that finally eludes him. The protagonist searches for an answer that will give him immortality, a victory over suffering and death. Gilgamesh ends frustrated and empty. At one point he questions whether the gods are jealous of his beautiful friendship with Enkidou whose death he is mourning with inconsolable sorrow. At the end of the poem he sits naked on the ground by a river and weeps. He complains bitterly to the gods. Only they can enjoy life "under the sun" for humanity their days are counted, everything humans achieve is nothing but wind...

Gilgamesh, a legendary heroic king, represents Everyman for the Sumerians. He incarnates their values. This thoroughly hopeful outlook is contradicted by his inevitable and tragic destiny.

Another ancient poem, the *Enuma Elish,* also deals with the question of life and the human yearning for an answer. The same mythical language used in these two poems appears in the book of Genesis. It seems that the Jewish sages and priests who write Genesis borrow these myths from the Babylonians while the people of Israel remain in captivity in Babylon around the VII century B.C.

Pessimistic also is the explanation of the "drama of creation" in the *Enuma Elish,* the other poem found in Asurbanipal's library and which possibly dates to the XIX century B.C. This ancient poem recounts the beginning of creation, a creation caught between the forces of good and evil. Six hundred gods are aligned on each side of the battle: a combat of giants which keeps the world in constant conflict and agony. Life is a continuous battle with no meaning, not even an issue. The struggle between the forces of good and evil involves man only as a victim.

At the summit of mount, dwells and dominates Mardouk, who could be Zeus. He is the supreme god, sun and light, warmth and life. But his domination is precarious because he cannot do anything against the forces of evil, against enemies of humanity. From the very beginning this *Supreme Being* has his hands tied behind his back. He wants to help humans, but he cannot deliver them from evil, suffering, and death. Faithful humans would sing to the unachieved victories of Mardouk and would offer him their oldest sons or their most beautiful virgins in sacrifice. Maybe placating the evil gods would help to avoid more punishment and suffering.

Sumerian thinkers generally have a pessimistic vision of human destiny. In both the *Gilgamesh* and the *Enuma Elish* man appears as a loser. No matter what he does, whether he is kind, strong, handsome, just, and loving, whether he is fighting to liberate the oppressed or against the most monstrous evil god, Gilgamesh, symbol of man, finds life a disappointing desert. All that awaits him at the end is inevitable death. The only way to cope with this bleak ending seems to be to unite in mutual fraternal bonds. If we must suffer and die, let us be friends and brothers through this ordeal. That seems to be vaguely suggested as the moral of Gilgamesh and Enkidou.

In summary, most ancient civilizations find only a few consolations in life. In the face of such tragic view of life, man's short consolation comes from fraternal solidarity with the rest of humanity and from trust in ephemeral victories of his benefactor gods. Against these minor consolations stands the appalling reality of man's tragic destiny; his progressive and inevitable destruction which ends in the corruption of death.

Most great ancient civilizations generally presented a bleak vision of man and the universe and an unclear purpose to life. The problem of suffering and death presents a stumbling block to any positive theory of a purpose in life. Nevertheless, they seem to agree on man's basic desire to live and to grow towards a somewhat more integrated and "transformed" human being who becomes more aware and more in touch with his life in the universe.

## 7) THE HEBREW

*An unprecedented and unique view of life.*

At about the same time as these ancient cultures proposed such pessimistic views of life, an author has the incredible audacity and certitude of faith to address his god this way in a Psalm:

> *"You will not abandon me your faithful*
> *to suffer the corruption of death"*
> Ps. 16:10

With a totally unprecedented view, the Hebrew people aware of the conflicting forces that seem to be manipulating History affirm the contrary to what all other civilizations affirm. The Jewish authors of the Bible are not naïve or ignorant about human frailty. The Hebrew people are in touch with human desolation of man in this world.

Despite a history which dates back to 1850 B.C (XIX century B.C.), full of tragedy, captivity, failure, and frustration, they offer a surprisingly positive and hopeful view of life. They affirm and proclaim with conviction that life is definitely directed to positive accomplishment.

*Then the eyes of the blind man shall be opened and the ears of the deaf unstopped; then shall the lame man leap like a hart, and the tongue of the dumb sing for joy. For waters shall break forth in the wilderness, and streams in the desert; the burning sand shall become a pool, and the thirsty ground springs of water.*
Isaiah 35: 5-7a

Salvation is the end of this life and hope is the helpful companion of the suffering man because God orders everything towards goodness.
God did not make death, and he does not delight in the death of the living.
For he created all things that they might exist, and the generative forces of the world are wholesome, and there is no destructive poison in them; and the dominion of Hades is not on earth. For righteousness (Justice) is immortal. Wisdom 1:13-15
This blunt statement is unique among the ancient civilizations. The direction of life according to the Jewish outlook on life is positive and hopeful despite the conflictive struggles of creation. There shall be peace on earth, and no more chaos, harm, or destruction! There is hope in life for man and creation!

*The wolf shall dwell with the lamb, and the leopard shall lie down with the kid, and the calf and the lion and the fatling together, and a little child shall lead them. The cow and the bear shall feed; their young shall lie down together; and the lion shall eat straw like the ox. The sucking child shall play over the hole of the asp, and the weaned child shall put his*

*hand on the adder's den. They shall not hurt or destroy in all my holy mountain; for the earth shall be full of the knowledge of the Lord as the waters cover the sea.*
Isaiah 11: 6-9

Where does this unique vision come from?

Many authors agree that this positive vision comes from the profound experience of that "living" god or "god of life" that the Jewish people claim they have been gradually discovering through their history. The intensity with which they experience that discovery is such that it makes them boldly contradict their own human experience of suffering and death and the affirmations of all the other religions and civilizations. The climax of their discovery is *their own belief in an all powerful, infinitely merciful God, author and friend of a creation that He himself has willed.*

Around the year 700 B.C. and on, they begin to feel so bold about their conviction that their positive view is even enlarged in the Bible to encompass not only Jewish history but also the history of all humankind. This universal vision comes more noticeable between the years 500 and 400 B.C. Paradoxically all this begins to happen during the captivity under the Babylonians when they are in a time of shame, not glory. It is time for reflection and maturation, a time of wisdom for the people of Israel. They have time to reflect on their past. The prophets, priests and sages put together all oral tradition and compose their history in the light of the awareness they now posses. They must share their unique vision of life with their own posterity and all the other civilizations with which they are coming in contact. The Jewish people are becoming more universal in their wisdom. Everyone, they believe, should know the history of that incredible relationship between God and the chosen people.

*Everyone should know their interpretation of the mystery of life and the universe in the light of the relationship they have found to exist between God and humankind.*

Doubtless, history brings to us the fundamental questions of life through ages of human experience. We can study how man has dealt with the mysteries of life in himself, in his social awareness, and in his ways of interpreting the universe. That humans desire to live, despite suffering and struggles, is a fact of history. Their desire to transcend, to go beyond their own physical and natural limitations, against all odds, is also proven by their anguish expressed in the history of literature and art to this day.

The ancient civilizations deal with the fundamental questions of life. Even though a fatalistic and pessimistic view of life pervades most of them, they find answers that confirm at least these two points: man's desire to live and his desire for transcendence. They find answers to help them live even if these answers are merely ideal fantasies to escape from man's terrible fate.

The Jewish people, nevertheless, offer a unique and refreshing answer that is not escapism from reality. The depth of the Jewish answer is intriguing and worth pondering because it seems to be based on man's universal quest for transcendence of suffering, and death.

No one can deny the enormous influence that the Jewish religion had in the Roman Empire at the peak of its power. The Roman Empire is also considered to be the convergence of many sources which launched Western civilization. The Jews contributed their religion to Western civilization with the Judeo-Christian faith. Although some would deny the name "Christian" to contemporary Western civilization, Christianity has certainly given the main direction to the history of the Western world. Because of the Jewish influence this unique vision of man in the universe and in relationship to God has undoubtedly prevailed. Western man grows by these beliefs and furthermore has kept developing and integrating this vision into the flow of his experience, into his growing awareness of the universe, and into his insights about the future.

*Thus, let us investigate in the history of the Jewish people how they discovered that unique positive vision of life. They left us with a singular document in which they recorded their process of awareness through the centuries.*

## 8) A UNIQUE HISTORICAL DOCUMENT

*A document about the human being in evolution.*

The Bible is a unique document, unprecedented and unparalleled by any work of history of such amplitude. It is a unique historical document that records not only the experiences of a growing civilization but also the reflections on these experiences.

The material in it was elaborated and transmitted in oral form over a long period of time. Eventually the different parts were composed, put together, and finally written into the one Book. The documents it contains were mainly rooted in oral traditions passed from generations to generations for hundreds of years. The stories were rich in content and the images used to express the relevance of their meaning. These stories covered more than 2000 years of history.

One of the reasons for its uniqueness is the relevant difference with other works of history. Most histories of the great ancient civilizations are usually heavily influenced by political leaders and heads of state at whose commands historians did their work. Also these other histories are written during the peak times of these civilizations and, therefore, recount the successful moments which they want kept for posterity.

The Jewish document, by contrast, is written in the language of the different social classes of the people of Israel, from the common fellow, the "anawim" to their leaders, judges and kings, through their brave women like Judith and Esther, and their rural housewives like Noemi and Ruth. It expresses the thoughts of their poets and sages and also the practical ingenuity of their leaders. It tells of their military conquests (usually modest) and also the shame of their losses, the times of wealth and glory, as well as the times of ignominious captivity. The Bible becomes an extraordinarily objective witness to the growth of a civilization.

But the most peculiar feature of this history is the *reflection* process that occurs within the written document. The history of the Israelites in itself reveals the growth of awareness of a whole people as they march through history and reflect on their past.

The Bible, in truth, is an anthropological source as it follows the concrete man, living in a group and considered in his dynamic course toward the future.

This "group", the Hebrew people, has very special characteristics. There is a peculiar fusion between the *national* (ethnic) and the *religious* in the history of Israel, especially in the Old Testament.

Their history is *not only Hebrew*. There is a slow obvious evolution form the Hebrew nomad society in the times of the Patriarch, passing through the Israelite society under the Judges and the Kings, to the final Jewish society after the exile. The influences and character borrowed from the many neighboring civilizations with which they came in contact, and which they integrated into their own civilization cannot possibly be extracted and isolated in that historical process. Their anthropological process is *not only Jewish*. Judaism evolves through the history of Israel. One can follow different currents and divisions throughout the Old Testament. Perhaps the dramatic division comes with the Christian era when a radical bifurcation occurred: the Jewish current and the Judeo-Christian current. Christianity continues the *evolutionary process* into the New Testament with a new light, but basically in the same tradition.

It is very difficult to understand the Bible as a whole because a book written by many writers with different styles and mentalities. We need to understand the languages and literary styles of an oriental whose modes of expression are different from ours 25 or even 30 centuries later. The ancient oriental concept of history is different from the factual narratives of western historiography.

Orientals employ allegorical literary creations which the western mentality would never accept as historically "true". *Midrashic* style, for example, is frequently used in the Old Testament as well as in parts of the New Testament. Midrash is a reflection based on minimal historical events, with a reconsideration of preceding scriptural events. It is designed to express a meaning or transmit a message that does not have to be strictly historical. The importance lies in the meaning of the message itself, not in the actual historical happening: what counts is the teaching behind the story.

Images are another important point that must be taken in consideration in the study of the Bible. Having been transmitted for hundreds of years by oral tradition, these stories had to be simple and at the same time rich in imagery, so that the message and the teaching, were clear and not easily forgotten. We must also remember that psychology is a very modern science and psychological moods would have been very difficult to express in words in ancient times without colorful images. What better image could have been found to express Jonah's psychological depression, after he runs away from his call and duty, than to be swallowed by a whale?

In summary, the Bible, being a document of the historical testimony of the human being through centuries of experience, constitutes an invaluable instrument for our search for answers to the fundamental questions of life. The Bible expresses a universal interpretation of life that is both actual and meaningful today.

We can definitely find answers in the Bible from the growing people of Israel, through the experiences of centuries. We can learn about our purpose to life, and the possibility of freedom through that process of consciousness, and finally, our responsibility in regards to the success or failure of our lives.

The Bible serves us no less than it served the Jewish as a manual to find answers in our own process of *conscientization* during life. We can find in the Bible our own purpose to life in that personal evolution, the possibility to be free through that process, our responsibility in the success or failure of our lives, and finally to find that happiness we all yearn.

## CONCLUSION PART I

In our search for happiness we have met recent thinkers and writers who in the midst of our apparently superficial modern world, have invited us to stop and reflect. Our Western civilization seems to have been deprived of the profound inner development the oriental civilizations have worked in history. The Jewish process that at one point in history injected a unique faith and vision to the whole world must make us stop and think. A true major clash of historical significance must have occurred. How this oriental way of believing irrupted the Greco-Roman rationalistic way of thinking. The Jewish mentality with its intuitive sensitivity for dreams, allegories, and signs must have had an over powering impact in the Roman world.

This impact would necessarily have caused theoretically a true synthesis and the enrichment of new way of life. However, the faith in that loving God who wanted us humans to love one another and build his kingdom of peace and justice, went through a longer process of integration. This faith had to be explained to the Roman world in terms of concepts and essential definitions, losing some of its initial spiritual strength. Christianity, thus, on impact, lost some of its freshness.

That is why we must avail ourselves of that Jewish faith-tradition that brought us the only positive vision of life. That unique vision which regardless all the struggles through European history, it still prevailing in the Western mentality.

---

*Let us follow the people of Israel through their history in the Old Testament. Le us try to understand why and how they were able to find a positive vision based on hope for all humanity. Our curiosity will take us through the different stages of awareness they experienced, their process of conscientization. Surely their growth in consciousness can be of help to our own individual and personal process in the midst of an also growing universal society. Maybe Israel can help us find the way to happiness.*

# PART II

# HISTORY OF THE GROWING HUMAN CONSCIOUSNESS

The Bible follows both the development of a civilization and the dynamic growth of the individual in that civilization. The Biblical man, let us call him *Israel*, discovers and becomes aware of his own reality and the universal reality that surrounds him.

Through different stages Israel, the human being of the |Bible, grows and matures into deeper and higher dimensions. As Israel integrates experience and reflection in a synthetical progression, he will find more mature answers about his purpose in life and the purpose of the universal.

Gilles Cusson, S.J. studies the process of awareness which the Jewish people experience in their history recorded in the Bible. Cusson's studies of biblical anthropology and his dynamic approach have been acclaimed by the Pontifical Biblical Institute of Rome, as the approach that really finds the substance of the Bible. According to Cusson there is an obvious evolution of consciousness in the people of Israel. We will use this anthropological interpretation to explain how the people of Israel discover through their history these positive answers so unique among the ancient cultures. Following their trajectory in history we may find answers to our own fundamental questions.

Throughout their history we can observe their religious and their national consciousness growing intermingled together. The process begins with the *individual* as a point of departure: Abraham, Isaac, Jacob, Moses. The process moves toward the *collectivity*: they become the people of Israel through the desert experience. In a pedagogical process, the individual, reflecting on his past, discovers gradually, from that communal sense of history, his own personal purpose in life. The prophets will contribute to that personal spiritual awareness.

We must distinguish between the terms personal and individual. "Individual" is a member of the collectivity. The term implies oppositeness to collectivity. The term "personal," on the other hand is used to stress the interior character of the person's awareness.

The history of Israel goes from the *national* to the *universal*: a result from reflection on that evolution that occurs through the different historical stages. The individual, at the same time, through that personal reflection, learns and grows in a process of spiritualization that ends in the universal man.

The process begins with the individual awareness in the **patriarchs**. They experience a growing understanding of God. Through this individual experience they become more aware of themselves and their role in the universe. Their awareness of God, especially in Abraham and Jacob, is not static but dynamic; it keeps growing and making them more intimate and close to God and his designs. The patriarchs are the leading figures in a growing relationship between God and the human being that develops through different aspects and becomes national and even universal. Anthropologically speaking, it seems that the human being discovers God by having different and deeper perceptions as man grows in life and history. These perceptions, recorded in the Bible, constitute an extraordinary document for posterity. The Patriarchs become so convinced of the uniqueness of their God that from then on their history, socially, politically, and personally, is forever centered on that God.

Jewish history develops from the patriarchs to the people as a national sociological phenomenon. The patriarchs' individual faith eventually becomes the faith of the national community in the Exodus through the desert with the leadership of Moses.

The process continues with the appearance of the **prophets**. They are the "stirrers" of consciousness in times when consciousness seems to remain stagnant after the Jewish people get settled in the promise land. The prophets call their people to personal responsibility. They help their people realize the personal commitment God demands in their relationship with him and with one another.

This deeper awareness finally becomes understood in universally comprehensibly proportions when the **sages** of Israel are able to articulate, the faith they have inherited from the patriarchs. This last stage of development seems to integrate all their history into one clear message of life and hope.

*It is helpful, at his point, to apply Teilhard de Chardin's process of personalization to the Hebrew historical process of consciousness. This application can help us to understand our own personal process. We will follow the history of Israel through the different stages explained by Teilhard: Centration, Decentration, and Super-centration.*

*Through Gilles Cusson's anthropological approach and Teilhard's stages of personalization we may be able to better comprehend the rich historical process of the Jewish people and its universal importance for us today.*

## 9) CENTRATION

*"Israel" gets to know itself while knowing God, its protector.*

### ABRAHAM
*Growing in self-confidence by trusting God and becoming aware of his universal responsibility.*

The story of Abraham, no doubt, was composed in the *midrashic* style, as we have already studied, based on an historical reality but "adorned" with colorful details of its times and culture.

Abraham was a wandering Aramean who migrated north from Ur of the Chaldeans going up the river Euphrates towards the region of Canaan. He lived in the nineteenth century B.C., maybe around 1850 B.C.

Abraham believed in an ancestral God who was more powerful than all the other gods. Cusson defends the theory that God's revelation follows the natural evolution of the human being without forcing his ways. By becoming aware of their life and personal experiences, human beings welcome God's revelation which is already acting upon creation in a movement of personal and universal evolution. Abraham becomes aware of the Highest God who had been revealing himself to him.

The oriental conception of history brings a multitude of images and symbolic concepts to express an idea. The book of Genesis describes moods and inner reflections of human beings with striking images. Most of these visual descriptions seem to be expressing a totally internal experience lived by the Patriarchs. They do not have to describe external objective historical facts.

Abraham becomes aware that God is communicating with him. Dialogue is established between them, and the relationship appears to be growing in a process of continuous discoveries through their awareness. The account of the Covenant between Yahweh and Abraham (Gen. 15) is certainly the starting point, the beginning of a true friendship and the center and pivot of the history of Israel. Abraham has already received a call from God to risk, to leave everything behind and to go to the new land God will show him. The promise is there: "*I will make you a great nation, and I will bless you; I will make your name great, so that you will be a blessing*" (Gen. 12: 2).

The idea of receiving a blessing from God enjoys tremendous importance in the history of Israel. Abraham feels overwhelmed with joy and humility over such an honor.

Later, with the episode of the covenant, Yahweh takes Abraham outside late at night and shows him the stars, "*Look up at the sky and count the stars, if you can, just so shall your descendants be*" (Gen. 15: 15). Yahweh promises him a child!

Nevertheless, at the time that Abraham receives the Promise, questions arise and create conflicts on the way. Sarah, his wife, was barren. To stress that fact, the book of Genesis presents Sarah as an old woman over sixty-five, a fact that seems contradictory to the episode in Egypt when Abraham tells her: "*I know well how beautiful a woman you are. When the Egyptians see you, they will say, 'She is his wife'; then they will kill me, but let you live. Please say, therefore, that you are my sister...*" (Gen. 12:11-12). Abraham knows a God that is powerful, but he does not know all this at once. He discovers

God's power gradually. Through this episode he discovers that his God is even powerful with the Egyptians.

Sarah's living in the Pharaoh's palace and subsequent calamities arouse suspicions among the Egyptians. Abraham has to tell the truth and blames the calamities on his God's being displeased at Sarah's situation. Struck Abraham comes to the realization that his God is very powerful, even more powerful than the gods of the Egyptians.

There is a second instance in which Abraham seems to be surprised by God's power. Abraham has been promised a child. Sarah herself is the first one to advise him to take her slave maid Hagar and have a child with her as Sarah cannot bear children. Abraham seems to expect no miracles from God even though God has promised him a child, so he takes the most natural course. The slave should bear his child. Finally, Sarah becomes pregnant. Both Sarah, who was supposedly ninety years of age at the time, and Abraham who was a hundred – surely symbolic figures – (Gen. 17-17), praise the Lord for this wonder. They both have grown in awareness. Yahweh, their Lord, is indeed powerful!

Abraham's faith increases with every new discovery, in every new reflection on the experiences of his life. He is forever the prototype of the faithful man. When God calls Abraham responds in faith. Abraham becomes increasingly sensitive to God's communicating with him through signs. He believes that God is constantly communicating with him through everything around him. In his dreams or in his sleepless vigils at night, or through watching the stars Abraham tries to hear the many ways in which God communicates with him. Through all the events of his life God has been revealing something new to him. Abraham responds to every call with a burning desire to be ever more faithful to his God.

The episode of Isaac's sacrifice is probably Abraham's most profound experience. Abraham believes that whatever happens in the future will eventually be better for him. He puts everything in the hands of God. This new "call" he believes to be coming from God, it not only demands a response that implies a break with his past and risk, but also demands a new risk: his future and the promise itself.

Cusson explains Abraham's test in the same anthropological approach. God uses experiences in Abraham's life and the world around him in order to test his fidelity. At that time many neighboring civilizations practice human sacrifice to their gods. Abraham may feel that he can show faith in his God by doing the same. If all the others show their faith to their gods by offering them their oldest son, should he not prove his faith in the same way? Nevertheless, in Abraham's case this would be the end of his future and the future of his descendants.

In his internal anguish Abraham opts to be faithful to Yahweh by what he thinks is the proper thing to do – as all the others do to their lesser gods. Yahweh, nevertheless, stops him before he can kill Isaac, and praises Abraham's fidelity.

This experience does not end with a reward. (He has trusted in the God of life, not in a god of death.) Abraham understands God's relationship with him to be a real friendship, not based on reward and punishment. The test brings Abraham to a new dimension in his friendship with Yahweh. Abraham now understands and enjoys a new and deeper intimacy with his God. He has become aware of what life is all about: to risk, to advance and progress, to trust and to hope.

In our covering the story of Abraham in the light of Teilhard de Chardin's process of personalization, we realize and amazing comparison. Abraham may be understood to represent the child who tests and is tested by his parents through his childhood. As he grows, he becomes more aware of life and his surrounding world. He learns through personal experience or through the teachings and guidance of his parents. The child discovers his parents' love and begins to trust them at a very early age. Their love means protection and care for him. He begins to understand that he must grow, risk, and learn through life. He must move on in this world, overcome fear, observe, and act. He becomes aware that he must reflect constantly on what is happening in him and around him. Abraham, indeed, is Everyman, each one of us as we discover God, the universe, and the meaning and value of life.

## JACOB
*Awareness of a deeper truth in life.*

Jacob appears in the book of Genesis as the prototype of the young, impetuous, and adventurous. He feels so sure of himself that, advised by his mother (Gen. 27), he plays a trick on Isaac to get his father's blessing which he has acquired from his brother Esau (Gen. 25). That blessing makes him the heir of the promise given by God to his forefathers. Jacob has to flee the wrath of Esau, and in doing so, two major internal experiences change his life, which will make him infinitely more aware of his role in history and his call in life.

At Bethel, Jacob has a dream. The time has come now for the fugitive to perceive a deeper truth. In his dream Jacob sees "a stairway resting on the ground with its top reaching to heaven; and God's messengers were going up and down on it" (Gen. 28: 12). Jacob becomes aware that he is in truth now the recipient of the promise, as were his father Isaac and his grandfather Abraham. The experience of this night was much more than an inner consolation for Jacob. Something has happened: a revelation of God has occurred that would affect his spatial and material world. He receives the blessing of Yahweh, the God of his ancestors. "Know that I am with you," says the Lord (Gen. 28: 15). Jacob understands this dream to be the confirmation of his role in life: to be an agent of God in history. This becomes clear in the dream, there is no such thing as "the gods up there" and the poor-human-slave-victims down here as most neighboring civilizations believed. Jacob understands that there is an open communication between God and the human beings. The messengers (angels) go up and down the stairs that link heavens and earth.

This is his first major interior experience. The second comes some years later. Jacob is called by God to return to his land and to stop running away from Esau "Return to the land of your fathers, where you were born, and I will be with you" (Gen. 31: 3). He is afraid and confused. He trusts God, but the unknown future and the danger involved make him feel anguish and great fear. Then comes his second great experience of awareness.

At Penuel, Jacob is left alone. "Then some stranger wrestled with him until the break of dawn" (Gen. 32: 25). Jacob wrestling with the Angel visualizes the fight against temptation, the most profound temptation Jacob has ever felt in his life. He is tempted to give up, to avoid facing his threatening future. This encounter was understood as a test of Jacob's fitness for the larger tasks that lay ahead. The results were encouraging. Though he was left alone to wrestle through the night with a mysterious assailant, Jacob did not falter. The stranger, at one point in the match, is revealed to Jacob as God himself.

To his astonishment Jacob understand God as his challenger, a friendly contender who is testing his strength and intelligence. Jacob is wrestling with God, provoked by God himself! He understands immediately the meaning of this experience. Must he confront a threatening future and the uncertainty that could bring him danger even death? Or could he not run away and settle comfortably somewhere else? After this experience the answer is clear. Jacob already knows the higher role he has been called to fulfill. He must trust his God. Yahweh is always with him. Penuel has given Jacob this reassurance. He has been invited to be an agent of destiny. He knows he is free to decide.

Finally, Jacob returns to the land of his fathers to face his brother and the future. He accepts the risk.

It is indeed fascinating to note the number of artists, painters and sculptors, who have chosen to work with this theme of Jacob wrestling with the Angel. No one can deny the strange fascination which the theme of the human being wrestling with God can exercise on us, the questioning struggling human beings. The theme can suggest anything from our wrestling with nature and the elements, to our wrestling with life in general, or even our wrestling with ourselves. All these interpretations are true. As Jacob becomes aware that life is a challenge, that nature, "the others", and God himself are constantly challenging him to become more of a person, so this is true for each of us. Jacob understands that living is to risk, to move forward, to become God's agent on earth for the sake of humankind.

Nevertheless, Jacob's experience goes much deeper. John Navone, S.J., professor at the Gregorian University in Rome, remarks on the importance of Jacob for the people of Israel and also for all of us humans. For this chosen people Jacob is both an historical individual and a corporate personality symbol of their own relationship to God. In Jacob-Israel they recognize their own wayward nature. They know they have not deserved God's favors. It is God's own loving will, a real gift. They have no claims on God; they cannot "force His hand" with human effort. Jacob was not chosen because he was righteous. He is righteous because he is chosen. The people of God humbly realize that God has not chosen them because of their own qualities or goodness. They well know how unfaithful they are. God loved Jacob, and the ground of His love lies solely in His own goodness, not in the virtues of Jacob.

Above all, Jacob is the symbol of Israel's own humble hopes, dreams, and aspirations. And because he continues to hope, he becomes the hope of all the nations who would receive God's blessing through him.

Jacob becomes the image of *everyone* in the western thinking. The limited fragile human being is chosen by God to be an agent, the instrument of salvation!

This is neither a pessimistic, nor a naïve view of human life. It does not ignore our life long struggles. It is the realistic view of human beings always facing life. This attitude towards risk was unknown in Jacob's time. Like Gilgamesh, human beings were losers and victims of the gods. They could only sit empty handed and naked to weep bitterly their misfortunes.

Jacob redeems the figure of Gilgamesh who until that moment had been the representative of the human condition, the universal man. In Jacob humankind wins the friendly fight with God his challenger, because God has assured us, "I will be with you always... to protect you". Now we know that we can let ourselves be guided and follow our Best Hope

Jacob represents all of us in our discovering our best possibility, our willingness to accept the challenges and risk of our human adventure.

---

*This audacious representation of God as a challenger offered in Jacob's personal history gives us a new understanding of life. Jacob is definitely source of encouragement through our own struggles and difficulties.*

---

## 10) DECENTRATION
*Israel's individual experience becomes collective experience.*

### MOSES
*Spiritual guide of the people of Israel*

Moses communicates the personal religious experience ot the patriarchs to the people of Israel. Like the patriarchs, Moses receives a personal call and confirmation from God. Like Abraham and Jacob, Moses is blessed by Yahweh who talks to him face to faith. But Moses receives a different call. He is invited to be the spiritual leader of the people of Israel, to make them a nation, thus communicating his own individual religious experience to them collectively.

Moses lived around the year 1225 B.C. As we are already familiar with his early life, we will concentrate on his life as a young adult life.

During the times of Moses thousands of Jewish slaves worked for the Egyptians under dehumanizing conditions as construction workers. Moses, through brought up as an Egyptian, is a Jew. He continued to have a strong feeling of identification with his Hebrew Kinsmen, as is shown vividly by his impulsive action on seeing an Egyptian Taskmaster beating a Hebrew slave. (Ex. 2:11- 15) After killing the Egyptian Moses flees for Madian. There, in the desert a deeper religious experience begins with his spiritual awakening. He is certainly aware of the suffering of his people, even though the Egyptian system was favorably to him personally. Moses now becomes aware of deeper values in his life. This is when Moses receives God's call (Ex. 3: 15).

Moses meets Yahweh face to face at the mountain of God in Madian, a sacred place as Bethel was for Jacob. The striking image of the burning bush expresses vividly and symbolically the internal reality of the formidable encounter Moses experiences with God. God calls and reveals himself to Moses in a burning fire that keeps burning without consuming the bush!

The following dialogue which takes place between Yahweh and Moses is one of the richest dialogues between God and man in the history of Israel. God tells Moses:

> *I have witnessed the affliction of my people in Egypt and have heard their cry of complaint against their slave drivers, so I know well what they are suffering.* (Ex. 3: 7).

Yahweh is concerned for the Israelites, and he calls them "his people" for the first time in history. In Abraham's life they have already known he is a just God, but in Moses' life the people of Israel get a new view: Yahweh is God of Justice, of human justice, of social justice. This understanding is unique among all the ancient civilizations in which arbitrary gods oppressed hopeless human beings.

> *Therefore, I have come down to rescue them from the hands of the Egyptians and lead them out of that land into a good and spacious land, a land flowing with milk and honey.*
> (Ex. 3: 8)

Very few civilizations at the time represent their gods as just and fair. Usually the gods are depicted as arbitrary and unpredictable as human beings can be. This idea of the God of justice prevails from that moment on through Israel's history. Later, the law of Moses also shows the importance of this social concern as an issue directly inspired by their God.

However, God will not rescue the Jewish people himself. He asks Moses to be his emissary to the pharaoh. God wants Moses to be the leader of his people, to take the Hebrews out of Egypt and to direct the most spectacular large-scale educational training ever recorded in history. The tradition that begins with Moses was to continue throughout the history of the Old Testament: God inviting us human beings to carry out his designs. God asks for our cooperation. God "consults" us. He never forces us to cooperate with his plans, but persuades us to by giving us support: he will always be present. We humans alone appear to be making history.

First Moses, then all the prophets, receive God's call. They always seem to have an excuse at the beginning. Moses claims he stutters, he cannot express himself well. All of them argue with God. God wants a free response, but he is persuasive: *"Do not be afraid,"* he says, *"I am with you always"* (Ex. 3: 12). Still Moses resists with all kinds of excuses. He even ask God for his name. And here God then gives him the most astonishing revelation: He gives Moses his name: *"I am who I am"* (Ex. 3: 14), which in the metaphysical sense means causality. He causes to be what comes to existence. Some authors discover in the second "I" an implied future sense: I am who I will be. This interpretation holds that God wants to stress the permanence of his **presence.**

In that context, this definition resembles the words of confirmation and support God gives after every call. These words appear in the Old Testament after every call to the prophets. They also appear in the New Testament in the Annunciation of Mary and in the sending and farewell of the apostles at the Mount of Olives: I am with you. I will be with you until the end of times. Yahweh reveals himself as the faithful living God, always present to his people, and furthermore the God who cares and is deeply concerned about the suffering of his people: the God of Justice!

Moses becomes the spiritual leader of the people of Israel. They leave Egypt as a disorganized mass of people. Almost unwillingly they follow Moses and wander around the desert for many years. Some of them complain. Others plainly state that they want to go back, seeming to prefer slavery than freedom in the hardships of the desert. "But you had to lead us into the desert to make the whole community die of famine!"(Ex. 16: 3). The community does not die, instead they begin to realize a most striking phenomenon: they are a community now and they are beginning to become a nation! In the desert the people of Israel becomes educated, organized, and civilized. They are no longer slaves. They will no longer be nomads when they arrive at the Promised Land.

## THE LAW
*An exercise of responsibility: a direction in life.*

From the mount Moses brings them a Law. The people finally accept their law with pride because it means for them liberation and life. Now they can show all the neighboring civilizations that they are no longer uncivilized nomads or slaves. They have a law, a constitution. They are now a nation!

We must not overlook the fact that the law of the Sinai is especially directed to a still primitive and rebellious people. This law has to cover every domain: religious, moral, social, and political. As we can observe, for the Jewish people, law, nation, and religion are three aspects of the same reality. The law makes them a nation, a free nation depending only on their God. No longer do they call God "the God of our Fathers", now he is their God, the God of the people of Israel.

The law is written in the language of the covenant, as a friendly and loving relationship between God and the human beings. This sacred engagement" will demand an active and true fidelity on the part of Israel. God, in return, is and always be the God of his people.

We become aware that Moses elaborates the law from his spiritual and personal experience of encountering God. This law is guidance for the people, a direction for people to follow, a means to encounter God. Moses law is unprecedented. Compared with any of the legal systems of neighboring civilizations in which the concept of "law" usually meant the arbitrary will of the ruling class, compared with the religious rules of other civilizations which deal only with the rituals and sacrificial offerings to placate the wrath of the gods, the Law of Moses comes as a unique change in history. It has two dimensions: the *vertical,* which is "love and worship thy God," and the *horizontal,* which is "love and respect your neighbor." Both dimensions are expressed almost with the same emphasis and they are both referring to a relationship of love –with God and with one another. Love and not fear is the principle upon which this law is based. The idea of justice appears clearly as the true expression of the relationship with God and with others.

Personal evolution, as a form of religious experience, in the patriarchs is communicated and accepted by the people as a nation through a process of social identification that lasted for forty years in the desert. Moses led the people out of Egypt to freedom and through the freedom of law toward the future. In faith and hope the people of Israel arrive in the Promised Land after a long and painful but dynamic encounter with their *Living God* in the desert.

## 11) SUPERCENTRATION, SPIRITUAL INTEGRATION

*The appearance of the prophets and the conversion of the sages define the mature period of Israel.*

As Israel reaches maturity, its experience becomes more universal. Through a deeper and an internal personal awareness, a universal consciousness gives new light to the question of life. After the death of Moses the people of Israel led by Joshua settled in the Promised Land. The judges, Gideon and Samson, strengthened their identity as a nation. They undergo a period of institutionalization. This sociological phenomenon constitutes the last step in their process of communal identification. Just as when the adolescent becomes adult he must get settled. One must "fit" into a group within the large group. The law regulates the functioning of individuals and of the different groups with one another. The law also protects the individual from being absorbed by the group. There are rights and duties. Societies then are formed this way.

Institutionalization, however, can also bring stagnation. The Jewish people get their kingdom, their temple, wise kings, and even wealth. The luster of Solomon lures the queen of Sheba and other neighbors. After some years their own success blinded the people of Israel. They go astray, fights, divisions, political quarrels, and finally religious schism follow. The kingdom divided into two kingdoms, Judah and Israel (2 Chr. 10, 11). Then, the prophets appear to denounce the narrow-mindedness that has pervaded everything. They thunder against hypocrisy and infidelity accusing the people of Israel of having many gods and not being faithful to the God Israel. A real contradiction is the general way of behavior. On the one hand the Jews are obstinate about their rituals, practices, and religious rules. They do not miss a detail. But on the other hand their practices are empty. The spirit that has inspired the law is not there anymore. The love of God has disappeared. Their laws are merely written words; justice has been forgotten.

## THE PROPHETS
*Stirrers of consciousness*

The prophets are inspired men who respond to an authentic personal *vocation,* and take the word of God, their message, to the people. The prophets of Yahweh exercise the role of *raisers* of awareness or *stirrers* of consciousness, promoters of faith in the covenant and in the hope for the messianic promise. They appear in the time of the Kings when the role of chief of the people no longer coincides with the role of spiritual leader. However, it is not until the eighth century B.C. when the Major Prophets, that is, the writers-prophets, come on the scene.

The task of the prophets is to continue the spiritual itinerary after Moses and the Judges. Their action follows the evolutionary process of internalizing and spiritualizing the reality of the covenant. Globally, their task would consist of making the people understand that, beyond the issue of faithfulness to a contract, beyond the mere obedience to a law and the strict following of liturgical practices, the people were engaged in a "love story." The prophets come to show the people the true reality of an internal spiritual evolution, at the deepest core of which is the personal encounter with the God of life.

*"For it is love that I desire, not sacrifice."* (Hosea 7: 6)

There are two ways in which the people of Israel are being unfaithful: First, with a religious practice entirely external, formal, without soul.

> *Since this people draws near with words only*
> *and honors me with their lips alone,*
> *though their hearts are far from me,*
> *and their reverence for me has become*
> *routine observance of the precepts of man.* (Is. 29: 13)

Secondly, they are unfaithful with concrete idolatrous practices.

> *Their land is full of idols;*
> *they worship the work of their hands.* (Is. 2: 8)

This conversion, or better, the process of understanding a more profound sense of fidelity, implies a rediscovery of the covenant: the loving pact between God and man. The prophets make this fact so clear that they do not hesitate to speak of the matter as the conjugal love between husband and wife. Infidelity to the Covenant especially idolatry, will be referred to as adultery or prostitution. The striking image used by Hosea has no parallel in history. God is the husband, the people are his wife.

*On that day she shall call me 'my husband,' and never again 'my master.'* (Hosea 1: 18)

Hosea uses the drama of his own life to express his message. His prophecy is rooted in his own unfortunate marriage to Gomer, his unfaithful wife. Hosea's personal tragedy profoundly influences his teaching. In fact, his on prophetic vocation and message were immeasurably deepened by the painful experience of his married life.

Gomer, the unfaithful wife, symbolizes faithless Israel. Hosea's writings reveal a very sensitive, emotional man who can pass quickly from violent anger to deepest tenderness. And just as Hosea cannot give up his wife forever, even when she lives as a harlot, so Yahweh cannot renounce Israel. God would chastise, but it would be a chastisement of the jealous lover, longing to bring back the beloved to the fresh and pure joy of their first love.

> *"I will go after my lovers," she said,*
> *"who give me bread and my water,*
> *my wool and my flax, my oil and my drink.*
> *Since she has not known*
> *that it was I who gave her*
> *the grain, the wine and the oil,*
> *and her abundance of silver...*
> *Therefore I will take back my grain*
> *in its time,*
> *and my wine in its season;*
> *I will snatch away my wool and my flax,*
> *with which she covers her nakedness.*
> *So now I will lay bare her shame*
> *before the eyes of her lovers*
> *and no one can deliver her out of my hand.*
> *I will bring an end to all her joy. (Hosea 2: 7- 13)*
> *...So I will allure her;*
> *I will lead her into the desert*
> *and speak to her heart.*
> *From there I will give her the vineyards she had.*
> *...She shall respond there*
> *as in the days of her youth*

*when she came up from the land
of Egypt." (Hosea 2: 16- 17)*

The prophets not only denounce; they also announce. The message of Jeremiah, for example, speaks of a future change, an internal renewal.

*I will place my law within them,
and write it upon their hearts;
I will be their god,
and they shall be my people. (Jer. 31q: 33)*

It is through this theme of a renewed spirit that the prophets express their real message: the personal discovery of a true, internal fidelity to God, to his loving and his living relationship.

The prophets are preaching a message of hope announcing a hopeful future. The people of Israel must become aware of a deeper and personal relationship with a God who promises life. This promise will become a reality not only in human beings, but also in the whole of creation.

*Until the Spirit from on high
is poured on us.
Then will the desert become
an orchard. And the orchard be regarded as a forest.
Right will dwell in the desert
and justice abide in the orchard.
Justice will bring about peace. (Is. 32: 15- 17a)*

The message of the prophets transcends the present and the immediate future, to the eschatological future. Their hopes entail the *messianic promise* and the prophetic vision of salvation.

*Then will the eyes of the blind
be opened,*

*the ears of the deaf be cleared,
then will the lame leap like a deer
and the tongue of the dumb will sing. (Is. 35: 5- 6a)*

*He will destroy death forever.
The Lord Gold will wipe away
the tears from all faces;
the reproach of his people
He will remove
from the whole earth;
for the Lord has spoken. (Is. 25: 8)*

The prophets elicit a profound change that contributes to the maturation process of the people of Israel. Through them the people of Israel not only return to their God, but also sharpen their vision of the future. This future is presented now not in constrict nationalistic terms, but in a new universal vision. The people of Israel now understand themselves as part of the world with a mature vision and a message for all peoples in the universe.

## THE SAGES

*Deepening a universal vision*

Time passes and the message of the prophets finally filters down to the people. Of course, bad times occur again, and the captivity in Babylon makes the experts of the law reflect on deeper things than the written law. Aware of a deeper reality they rediscover the spirit they had lost and the vision of life. They recognize their mistakes and feel sorry for their infidelity towards God, who is still calling, giving them another chance.

First the prophets, later the sages, are capable of personalizing the true spirit of the law. The promise, the meaning of life, and the evolution of history, are all now seen under a new light, a deeper understanding: God's promise of salvation. They know that even after being unfaithful to the living God, his mercy is so great that he will keep the promise and always give them another chance. This is made clear by the priest writers in the scriptural interpretation of the "fall" of humanity in Genesis. Adam and Eve, the universal man, is given another chance.

The people of Israel are at the peak of their maturity. As mentioned earlier, this is the time when the Bible becomes a written document of their history. At this period, the time of the sages or of wisdom literature, a new *universal view* which comes from the prophets appears in their writings. They do not limit their concerns to the Jewish people only. They talk about "the just man", "the strong woman", the times and changes of the world. They give advice about how to grow in knowledge, how to lead a meaningful life. It is in this period that the Jewish people come out of their ethnocentricity and become part of the current world civilization. They are open to recognize the good in others. Even in religion, a Babylonian high priest, Melchizedek, who is not a Jew, is exalted as the prototype of the priest. The book of Proverbs, the book of Job, the book of Wisdom, the Psalms, the Song of Solomon, etc. all have been written for and about the universal man. They seem to announce that *real wisdom is profoundly human and profoundly spiritual*. The person is integrated totally in God's plan for salvation, actively involved in the world but at the same time looking for the future in the hope of eternal salvation.

The sages praise wisdom, *a human wisdom that leads naturally to God*. It seems at this stage that the Jewish people have integrated all things in life. The book of Sirach describes the human model as the spiritual person, humble and sincere, always seeking justice. The wise person is not presumptuous neither relies on wealth and power. The just person seeks true friendship and is responsible at home with his family. He is well-mannered and prudent. He does not judge people by the exterior of their appearance but listens to the poor man's wisdom. Health of mind and body are a blessing.

The book of Proverbs is also full of sayings of the wise. It offers advice about a virtuous life and warns about its perils. The honest man must be aware of the wicked. The ideal woman is praised for being strong and bright:

> *She is clothed with strength and dignity,*
> *and is free from anxiety about the future.*
> *She opens her mouth in wisdom*
> *and her tongue is kindly counsel. (Prov. 31: 25- 26)*
> *She reaches out her hands to the poor,*
> *and extends her arms to the needy. (Prov. 31: 20)*

The new wisdom is universal. All human beings must understand life and the world in this new consciousness. This wisdom, however, points to an eternal vision of life in spite suffering and death.

> *But the souls of the upright are*
> *in the hands of God,*
> *and no torment can touch them.*
> *To the unenlightened, they appear*
> *to die,*
> *their departure was regarded as*
> *disaster,*
> *their leaving us like annihilation;*
> *but they are at peace.*
> *...their hope was rich with*
> *immortality. (Wisdom 3: 1- 4)*

According to wisdom literature, the well integrated human person is someone who keeps in touch with his inner reality no less than with his external reality. The mature person possesses a universal vision, is a person of prayer and reflection, whose life is one of faith, hope, and love through every situation in life. Such person lives in a dynamic evolution, personally, communally, and universally. While fully human and independent, the mature person, according to the sages of Israel is truly humble and dependent of God.

*At this point in our quest for happiness we must pause, study, and reflect over a major obstacle we find that surmounts all true and sincere development to a positive vision of life: suffering and death.*

*Like all the ancient civilizations, Israel has to find an answer for suffering, more so since Israel, unlike most ancient civilizations, has presented such a positive outlook on life and man's purpose in life. Let us see how the Hebrew people are able to explain to us the problem of suffering.*

## 12) SUFFERING AND EVIL

*Negatives in a positive vision of life.*

Spiritual integration is not possible unless we confront with honesty the true reality of our existence. We have to face and integrate our problems and difficulties. It would be unrealistic to ignore the negatives we find in life. Today's media keeps offering all sorts of escapisms trying to keep us ruled by our instincts rather than reason. We definitely need to face the difficulties of life.

That is why Israel at the peak of wisdom has to confront and integrate the problem of suffering.

Suffering has been a difficult reality Israel has had to face throughout history. At this level of spiritual integration Israel must find a spiritually valid answer in order to integrate, probably the most difficult question Israel, like any other civilization, has ever confronted through his history. *Why is there evil and suffering in a creation that, as they maintained, is supposed to lead to life?*

Their living God, they claim, has given Israel an answer for life that goes beyond death. Creation is all very good, and man has a purpose in life: to live with all of creation and grow towards a final fulfillment in God. Israel's faith is deeply set along these lines. They must now confront the ultimate enigma: evil and suffering in life. This concrete and general presence of evil in creation constitutes a serious threat to faith in the living God as this faith rests necessarily on the positive statement of life. How can something that is apparently so evil be integrated into an overall positive outlook on life?

Most authors refer to these times as the peak of Israel's maturity. Paradoxically, these are not the times of fame, triumph, and wealth, but the times of the captivity in Babylon. The prophets, the priests and the sages work together to compose the one vision of their ancient history. In the light of their own history, the people are to interpret the whole history of humanity and creation in a universal view. At this point of universality Israel's maturity is such that they are able to integrate all the experiences of the past since the times of Abraham. They have become increasingly aware of God's relationship with man. They have grown to know the living God, the God of justice, the personal God.

In their maturity, the Israelites go back even to pre-history and explain creation, the fall of man, the tragedies of the world, and the problem of suffering. All this is interpreted in the light of Israel's solid faith and realistic hope, in a positive vision of life unknown to the rest of the world in those times

Two main styles of literature will be used to express the synthesis made by the prophets, the priests and the sages: the mythical language of Genesis, chapter one to eleven, and the wisdom language of the book of Job. The two will merge into the one language of "universalization."

Israel is now ready to confront the problem of evil and suffering. Through three main symbolic figures (none of them seem to be historical) who represent the "universal man," Israel tries to explain the problem as they deepen their understanding of life. Progressively Adam, Noah, and Job will pose three different views of the understanding of evil and suffering. Adam and Noah will deal with the evil in man. The book of Job will confront the tragic reality of the innocent who suffers.

## THE GENESIS' ACCOUNT OF EVIL IN CREATION

*"...and God saw that it was all very good"* (Gen 1: 31). With this statement, outrageous for those times, Israel narrates the creation of the universe. In times when all ancient civilizations believe that the sun, the moon and the stars were gods, the Jewish declare that a supreme God created the universe and each one of these "creatures" and not gods. For those civilizations creation was a negative force in which the human beings had to defend themselves like against an enemy. This positive view of the Jewish community of faith would have been unconceivable among the Babylonians from whom they "borrowed" most of the allegories of their creation narratives.

When in the beginning everything was chaos and disorder, God begins then his "process" of creation. This does not happen all at once. It takes "six days" for God to put the universe in order. These figurative numbers give us the idea that it was indeed a process in time. Teilhard de Chardin explains this evolution in its cosmic setting in order to understand the present situation of incompleteness and therefore to help foresee the ultimate completion in the future. Creation is given the power by God to grow, develop, and become ever more complete. At the end of this process stands fulfillment and real life. As Paul in his letter to the Romans declares, *"now creation groans in agony as if due to give birth... in its final fulfillment at the end of times."* ((Rom 8: 22). The real accomplishment of creation happens, therefore, in the eschatological future.

When man and woman are included in creation (created to be co-creators), they are given the task to help complete creation: to have dominion over the earth and its creatures (Gen 1: 28ff), to work and to make things grow: *"See, I give you every seed-bearing plant all over the earth."* (Gen 1: 29)

This lack of completion becomes a challenge to man who has been made to direct that evolving creation. The world, its elements, its sometimes uncontrolled forces all challenge man in life. He must find ways to control the elements, to develop science in order to transform the earth. Man must exercise his talents in the most creative way so he can fulfill God's will of exercising dominion over all things on earth. The task seems great. Many times the lack of goodness that has to be transformed and developed into goodness seems overwhelming. Man will experience that "lack of goodness" sometimes as *evil* or negative forces. Evil, the lack of goodness, must be overcome, organized, or transformed. Evil, then will be man's constant contender.

The Bible sets creation in those terms, but how to go about life in this constantly evolving creation? The answer, according the Jewish wisdom, is faith. This process in life necessitates a deep practical faith that can help man keep the vision of the future at all times. As Israel believes to be the real completion of creation, only faith in life and in the God of life will help man through the process. The Jewish community of faith believes nothing, not even the evil forces, will ever prevail against God's power. Israel, then, must always live in hope, a realistic hope towards the completion of life in creation.

## ADAM AND EVE
*Freedom in the human being*

Man and woman are invited to grow and develop with creation and to be agents of life. The human beings are free to evolve. Adam, like Jacob, wrestles with nature, with the threatening unknown, with his own insecurity, with incertitude and doubt. Soon he understands that the same lack of completion he has observed in creation is also within him. There are evil forces in him, as well. He must struggle and work. He must find and follow a practical way. Man must discover how to *become* in the right direction, how to build and not destroy, how to be positive and not negative. He discovers that the road is not so clear and distinct, once he begins moving. He must discern continuously in the light of the vision of faith. This is the challenge that freedom has posed in his life.

Temptation comes to Adam and Eve, prototypes of all humanity, as a rebellion against their own nature. They are creatures, they have been created by God to be fully realized in time, nevertheless, they react to their status and want to be absolutely independent. They want to be God *The serpent says: "... and you will be like gods..."* Gen 3: 5) and not just "created". Adam and Eve want a future according to their own design, overruling what God has designed for them. Their freedom turns them against themselves and against what they are, through the temptation of absolute self-determination.

From the symbolic story of the fall in paradise we come to the following observations. Adam and Eve, as participants of the "total human being" both decide against their status of "being created" which they enjoyed. God has invited them to be "co-creators" and assigned them to collaborate in the completion of an evolving magnificent plan. Nevertheless, they opt for a different direction from the one that demanded faith and trust in the future. By their decision they both renounce God's plan for their own fulfillment in time. They prefer the easily accessibly, good (or pleasure) for their immediate gratification, without consideration of the overall order of things. They would be like gods...! It has been the "side effect" of the freedom with which they were created.

According to the Bible, man's evil is attributed to human freedom. The human being is blinded by his own needs. Human freedom leads them astray. Adam and Eve are the prototypes for all humanity. Humans are imperfect and incomplete, therefore needy and poor. They must realize their own poverty. Only faith can help them accept it.

Gilles Cusson, through his thorough study of man and the Fall, affirms that after man's sin, creation continues to evolve the same as before by its own natural dynamic designed by God. But creation would now be imprisoned in its own natural being, and therefore, subject to corruptibility. Man would have to struggle even more now because he is conscious of his double inclination. His life will be a constant repentance and conversion as he realizes at every step the wrong choices he has made along the way.

The promise of life must become now stronger than ever as man is more aware of his need of a covenant with God faithful and alive.

We must remember that Genesis, especially the first chapters, is finally composed and arranged from early texts by the priests and the wise intellectuals, the sages, in the times of the Babylonian captivity. They are trying to explain the history of their people. Their main concern is to explain current suffering and captivity.

Why are they so unfaithful to a God who has proven his love and fidelity all along? Why are they captives in a foreign land when they were the recipients of the Promise? Why all the tragedies they have experienced in their history? What should they do?

The most interesting answer is clearly written between the lines. In spite of their unfaithfulness and evil ways, the promise is still alive. They firmly believe that their God is faithful to the covenant; that he is still beckoning creation and man towards the final fulfillment.

According to biblical views, all humanity shares the experience of the fall. All humanity represented in the symbolic figures of Adam and Eve, shares the ambiguity given by freedom. The narratives of the fall offer what seems to be a well thought, reflected upon, and realistic explanation of the human being in the face of evil. The ideal man created in freedom, in the image of God, capable of cooperating with God in the completion of creation, is defended with conviction. Nevertheless, the true ambiguity of man's life is exposed with honesty. If God's force pulls man toward goodness, man's narrow mindedness pulls him toward death.

From all this we can also view what the Judeo-Christian tradition calls *original sin* from a different angle. Cusson brings up Herbert Haag, whose studies defend the theory that no man enters the world a sinner. As a creature and image of God, he is from his first hour surrounded by God's fatherly love. Consequently, he is not at birth, as is often maintained, an enemy of God and a child of God's wrath. A man becomes a sinner only through his own individual and responsible action. The *inheritance* of Adam's sin means rather that sin, after its entrance into the world, is so spread that consequently all men are born into a sinful world and in this sinful world become themselves sinners.

The Jewish community of faith will affirm, with more intensity all the time, the role of faith in man's life. Through all the existing evil and in spite of it, God keeps his Promise. There will be violence, division, hatred, destructive wars, and death, but the man of God lives always in hope because Yahweh is the God of life. This hope has been confirmed through many centuries of stormy relationship with their living God. This is not the false hope of one who closes his eyes (or his mind) to avoid the horror around him and naïvely denies it. Israel has become maturely realistic through experience, history, and reflection.

## NOAH
*God confirms his faithfulness*

*"When the Lord saw how great was man's wickedness on earth, and how no desire that his heart conceived was ever anything but evil, he regretted that he hade made man on earth, and his heart grieved."* (Gen 6: 5) So the Lord sent a flood to wipe out everything he had created. The story of Noah seems to be non-historical, but it may be based in a real catastrophe. A flood is recorded, for instance, by the *Gilgamesh*. Utnapishtim tells Gilgamesh the story of a great flood of which he was the only survivor. Utnapishtim is saved by an ark he builds under the advice of the gods. In Noah's story, however, the story has a definite message. The flood symbolically represents all the physical and material evil in creation, those disorders of nature that must be confronted and controlled. The purpose of the whole story seems to be the reaffirmation that God is faithful to man and his creation, no matter what happens.

Some valuable observations can be made: First, God does not send the flood as punishment, but as purification. Secondly, Noah, a just and faithful person, is consulted about the problem. All around him there is destruction and violence, (Gen 6: 11), but Noah has been blameless and a good person. With Adam and Eve a pattern has already been set. There is always a hope for man, the sinner. God will always be faithful to him. Adam and Eve fail, Noah does not. In Noah's case the pattern is more than reaffirmed. God will always be faithful to the just man.

Noah represents Israel's understanding of the faithfulness of God to his creation. Israel becomes aware that in spite of evil and wickedness in man, God will be faithful.

The whole story of the flood is crowned at the end by the covenant God makes with Noah and his descendants (Gen 9: 1- 17) God establishes a new order in the world. There is always a beginning after purification. But most importantly, the covenant seems to be the seal of God's relationship with what remains of good, in spite of evil, in creation and man.

## JOB
*Suffering in the innocent*

Israel confronted the problem of evil in creation with a unique and positive vision, so different than the views of all neighboring civilizations. Evil has been analyzed in the stories of creation, Adam and Eve, and the Flood. Until this point the problem of suffering, as a consequence of evil, has been identified, in one way or another, with punishment for sin. Suffering usually appears as a consequence of man's disorderly conduct. Even in the later books of Exodus and Deuteronomy, the idea of suffering is usually related to punishment. The people of Israel are young and rebellious. Through experiences in the desert they need to understand the authority of God. Through punishment and reward they will learn to be faithful to God. This seems to be the awareness and understanding that the people of God can reach at this particular times. In this light they *interpret* God even punishing the children of their children in order teach his people to behave. They are growing in *consciousness*.

> *I the Lord, your God, am*
> *a jealous God,*
> *inflicting punishment*
> *for their fathers' wickedness*
> *on the children of those who hate me."* (Ex 20: 5)

The necessity of an ethical God is understandable, however, in those terms when the Jewish people are beginning to grow as a group through experiences in the desert. *Faith, a relationship of trust and hope, needs time to develop.* In time Israel will understand that their God is the source of life and hope, and that God's power of life exceeds by far all the powers of death and hatred. Therefore, the idea of punishment and reward is prevalent during Israel's "training." God blesses the faithful ones. When human beings became unfaithful and destroy the covenant, they deserve death.

As the People of Israel grow in experience and time, *they become aware of their relationship with God in totally different terms*. God is dealing with them on a level far beyond punishment and reward, on a level of mature love. The story of Adam and Eve already indicates that type of relationship. Even though their disobedience destroys their friendship with God, he gives them another chance. In the story of Cain and Abel, God punishes Cain but because of Cain pleas, God spares his life and protects him from being killed by others (Gen 4: 13- 14). God's mercy is such that he can skip punishment, even forgive the sinners or give them another chance.

Now, Israel, in a mature stage, has to face the **scandal** that has lingered for centuries in their tradition. The idea of punishment has been able to provide a *satisfactory* explanation for the presence of suffering in some cases but not in all lives. How can they *explain suffering in the innocent?*

The story of Job goes a long step ahead in the understanding of suffering. Job is the innocent and faithful man who does not deserve, by any means, any punishment. *"In the land of Uz there was a blameless and upright man named Job, who revered the Lord and avoided evil."* (Job 1: 1)

Job represents the universal man, as wisdom literature deals with the problem of suffering: in the child who is dying in pain, the good sick person prostrate in bed, the underprivileged suffering oppression. Job, the innocent man, becomes the victim of suffering.

Israel confronts the problem with astonishing honesty. The concept of the ethical God of reward and punishment seems to crumble.

Gilles Cusson declares that Israel, in Job, seems to contradict the 1300 year old experience they have of his living God. Job's suffering is as objective scandal for the people who hold the idea of God to be the ideal of justice, the God who rewards the just man and punishes the sinner. The story of Job goes beyond these simple terms. Job's fidelity appears to be tested. His suffering and his reactions or response are the focal point of Job's story. His condition stirs valid complaints about a system and a God who permits injustice. Job's friends in the story represent human reason in the face of suffering. Eliphaz argues with the silent Job and he listens to his friends. Their reasoning seems to make sense. What they say is all that human reason, in truth, can comprehend. Job responds to each one of them, nevertheless, with a deep-rooted faith that goes beyond human reason. Job accepts suffering as a fact of life.

Job is definitely not the naïve, ignorant faithful one. He is a well-educated man of experience and he knows what he means. Job's answer to his friends, expresses a valid complaint about the silence of God. He is indeed questioning God's justice, the justice of the God of the Covenant, toward the faithful man.

In the last chapters of the book of Job (38- 41) God speaks to Job and reminds him of past experiences through which man has become aware of God's power and transcendence. Job listens in awe. In his silence he understands everything with a fundamental and profound humility. As a result of this awareness, Job feels liberated and abandons himself to God and his power. Through this encounter with God Job is able to understand the mystery of life. As he feels part of a marvelous creation, he even forgets his own miserable condition.

God finally restores Job's health and prosperity, but the problem of suffering has not been solved. In the end the book of Job merely presents an attitude in the face of suffering. Job remains faithful beyond reason and logic. His hope in the Living God has given him the power to accept, to endure, and to live faithfully through suffering. Israel, the Biblical man, has learned by experience that he is growing and going towards the promise of life despite all evil and suffering. Hope is the force that moves the man of God through life and history.

Struggle, suffering, and the challenge of nature constitute the reality of the journey he has to face to complete creation and to reach the final fulfillment in God: true happiness.

## 13) A PREVIEW OF A NEW DIMENSION
*Suffering as Redeeming Love*

As we have followed Israel's thinking through the ages, we have become aware of the development in the understanding of a whole civilization. A mature Israel has been able to deal in all honesty with the problem of suffering. There is an obvious growth in understanding from the idea of suffering as punishment for the evil done, as expressed in Adam, to the idea of suffering expressed in the book of Job. As Paul Ricoeur points out, in Job's times the Hebrew vision of suffering is applied in a double standard. On the one hand sin deserves a just punishment of exile, as in the case of Adam, but on the other hand the suffering experienced by the innocent Job implies a terrible injustice. The growth of the concept of God from the ethical God has brought a seemingly inexplicable contradiction. An answer is needed to solve that conflict. Only the presence of a third figure, says Ricoeur, will announce the overcoming of that contradiction: this would be the figure of the "suffering servant" who will make of suffering an action capable of redeeming the evil done by man.

The book of Job has prepared the way for that mysterious suffering figure. The suffering servant of the prophet Isaiah opens a totally new and radical perspective on the meaning of suffering. It looks as if Israel's process of understanding has taken his people to a completely new awareness and consciousness.

The new meaning goes beyond the book of Job or any other explanation given by wisdom literature until that time. The Deutero-Isaiah, the second part of the book of Isaiah, is written (ca. 200 B.C.) two hundred years after the book of Job was written (ca. 400 B.C.). Through that period of time a new awareness has occurred in the life of Israel. Israel has deepened his awareness of God through the purification of wisdom and experience. **The "suffering servant" attributes to suffering a redeeming and liberating power.** Suffering can mean love, giving oneself to others. Suffering, according to Isaiah, is expiating for the sins of others and rescuing them from evil. The suffering of the "suffering servant" brings justice and forgiveness.

> *Here is my servant whom I uphold,*
> *my chosen one with whom I am pleased,*
> *upon whom I have put my spirit;*
> *he shall bring forth justice to the nations...*
> *...I formed you, and sent you*
> *as a covenant of the people*
> *a light for the nations.* (Isaiah 42: 1-9)

On Isaiah chapter 53 we find amazing revelations:

> *He was despised, the lowest of men,*
> *a man of sorrows,*
> *familiar with suffering...*
> *Yet ours were the sufferings he was bearing,*
> *ours the sorrows he was carrying...*
> *Whereas he was being wounded for our rebellions,*
> *crushed because of our guilt;*
> *... The punishment reconciling us fell on him,*
> *And we have been healed by his bruises.* (Is. 53: 3-5)

Isaiah announces a totally new dimension in our understanding of suffering and our understanding of life.

The interpretation of suffering in Job has been the most sensitive and positive we have received from any ancient document in history. Still, suffering, thus explained, seems to be a scandal, especially in the tradition of a people who claim to believe in the God of life. The scandal, although attenuated by the positive response of faith, and seen in the light of hope, is still a scandal.

Isaiah's Suffering Servant is the culmination of the positive and unique outlook of the Jewish tradition. This new concept involves the most profound analysis of love in its most intimate meaning: self-donation to the maximum. The long expected Messiah is announced and depicted as a suffering, tortured, and persecuted loser. The realization of the Promise, the messenger of God, would come as a loser for the sake of humanity: a victim of love. For the Jewish tradition, that statement in itself, must have appeared to be another scandal. Nevertheless, after following the growing, painful experience of the people of Israel through their history, the steady development of their awareness, and their process of maturation and integration, the Suffering Servant is perhaps the most outrageously logical product of reflective human experience. The Suffering Servant, the expiatory redeemer of humanity, marks the highest achievement in understanding in the Jewish outlook on life.

The idea of the Suffering Servant of the prophet Isaiah prepares the way to a totally new dimension of life and history.

> *Look, my servant shall prosper,*
> *will grow great, will rise to great heights.*
> *As many were aghast at him*
> *–he was so inhumanly disfigured*
> *that he no longer looked like a man–*
> *so many nations will be will be astonished*
> *and kings will stay tight-lipped before him,*
> *seeing what had never been told them,*
> *learning what they had not heard before.* (Is. 52: 13-15)

---

*It seems now obvious that in our search for happiness we must consider this new dimension found by the Jews in the history recorded in their Bible.*

*Our search for a way to happiness that would answer the questions of all human beings in all times, must now be defined in the mysterious and profound terms of the Suffering Servant of Yahweh, as contradictory as these terms may seem.*

---

## 14) THE IDEA OF GOD EVOLVING IN JEWISH HISTORY
*An incomprehensible relationship between God and man.*

By following the process of Israel's maturation through their history, we can also follow the development of an incomprehensible relationship between God and man. This development took centuries of history. Just as a child grows through the different stages of personalization, self-identification, social identification, and spiritual integration, the people of Israel discover God.

Throughout its individual, social, and universal growth, Israel gradually became aware of God in different and deeper dimensions through a dialectic process On the one hand, it's own history and experience, (objective pole); on the other hand, its reflection on that experience (subjective pole). Through the synthesis of the objective and the subjective man grows in consciousness. Furthermore, Israel makes another amazing discovery, far more profound and astonishing. At the same time that they gradually become aware of God, God on his part has been revealing himself to them in a mutual dynamic through their own history.

Abraham discovers the living God, his friend and protector, with whom he makes a pact, the covenant. This God appears to be calling him to risk, to leave behind the old ways, and to take new steps in life. Step by step Abraham confirms that his God friend is powerful, the most high of the gods. He is the God of life, not of death, a fact that Abraham understands through the test of his son Isaac. The "father" of faith responds with unconditional fidelity to Yahweh. Abraham is blessed and is constantly reaffirmed as the recipient of the promise.

Jacob meets the God of his fathers in a dream first, then, face to face as he wrestles with the angel. After he grasps the first revelation --an open communication with God-- the second one makes him comprehend what kind of God he is actually wrestling with: the challenger. Jacob understands and responds to the challenge, in deciding to risk, to move forward to the unknown and threatening future. He is sure now of his role in life as the father of the twelve tribes.

In Moses the people of Israel become aware (revelation through community reflection) of a new aspect of the living God. Now God is revealing himself as *the God of justice.* Yahweh plants his tent among them (Ex. 33: 7ff) and leads his people through the desert. God is finally understood by Israel as a people. He is the God of Israel who makes the covenant with man and who demands a twofold kind of love in return; love of God and love for one another.

The prophets point out the real intimacy in love that God wants and which his people seem to have forgotten. God is discovered, then as a loving God who wants to give and receive love. The prophets say God does not care for rituals or sacrifices. He wants personal commitment in love. The prophets underscore the twofold kind of love.

The prophets, the priests, and the sages of the mature Israel integrate all the aspects of God into one image. They will write the history of Israel as the love story between God and man, into one whole sacred history (Si. 44ff). Questioning and reflecting on their own history and tradition, the mature Israel unites all the stories, the poems, and the prayers as it becomes more deeply aware of God, his role in life and destiny. When the accounts of creation are composed, God is described as *God almighty,* the creator of the heavens and the earth. God creates man and woman in his own image and gives them the earth to work and exercise dominion over all creatures. God appears as a friend and walks through the garden with them. (Gen 3: 8)

At the peak of their integration stage, the people of Israel use the same ancient stories of creation used by other cultures. Israel's writers, however, give these stories a new meaning under the light of their experience and history. This knowledge of God has been growing slowly since the time of Abraham through the process of becoming a civilization. It seems as if in every new step of the process man has been discovering a new aspect of God and a deeper understanding of his presence. At the same time man becomes aware that God is all this time actively communicating with man, without forcing him or blocking his freedom, just like the murmur of the breeze, a tiny whispering sound, as God reveals to Elijah (I Kings 19: 12)

God has been giving clues about himself throughout history as the human beings become capable of understanding these clues. As the human beings mature, they need more clues and more aspects of God to reflect on. The child needs a loving protector, a father, a figure of authority as a guide, a God who would chastise him when he does not behave. Israel as a child cries to his God for help when the "bully" next door (the hostile nations around) beats him and abuses him.

> *Rise O Lord! Lift up your hand.*
> *Forget not the afflicted!*
> *Break the strength of the wicked*
> *and of the evil doer;*
> *punish their wickedness;*
> *let them not survive. (Ps. 10: 12; 15)*
> *May God come to my aid;*
> *may he show me the fall of my foes.*
> *O God, lay them, least they*
> *beguile my people.* (Ps. 59: 11- 12)

The adolescent Israel asks God for help to defeat his enemies.

*Fight, O Lord, against those who fight me! (Ps. 35)*

As Israel grows older and wiser, his prayer becomes mature and deeper: *"To you I lift up my soul, O Lord, my God. In you I trust!"* (Ps. 25). He asks for forgiveness when he has done wrong or when he becomes aware of his sinfulness (Ps. 51). And for guidance when confused (Ps. 25). His prayer of thanksgiving sings *"to the lord when he is happy"*. (Ps. 41: 30)

The more Israel finds wisdom, the deeper his prayer: *The Lord is my shepherd..." (Ps. 23). "As the hind longs for the running waters, so my soul longs for you, O God."* (Ps. 42)

In awe, Israel signs to his creator with the Psalm that must have inspired the authors who later composed the account of creation in Genesis.

> *Yahweh our Lord,*
> *how majestic is your name throughout the world!*
> *I look up at your heavens, shaped by your fingers,*
> *at the moon and the stars you set firm–*
> *What are the human beings that you spare a thought for*
> > *[them.*
> *Yet you have made man little less than a god.*
> *...Made him lord of the works of your hands,*
> *put all things under his feet,*
> *sheep and cattle, all of them,*
> *and even the wild beasts,*
> *birds in the sky, fish in the sea...* (Ps. 8)

It is the whole universe which receives the constant blessing of the Lord:

> *Praise Yahweh from the heavens!*
> *Praise Yahweh from the earth!* (Ps. 148)

## 15) A DEEPER MEANING FOR LIFE
*Man's purpose in life in the Old Testament.*

In conclusion, Israel, through its own experience, in the light of the God has discovered, has become aware of its own purpose in life. According to Gilles Cusson, it is clear in the Old Testament that *man exists to grow and to progress together with the universal creation toward fulfillment in God's plenitude.*

In its maturity, Israel understands three essential qualities about itself. First, it has been created "in the image of God" which means, man is a "creator being" the only creature capable of being creative.

Secondly, man accepts the real integral unity of his body and soul. Finally, he understands that he is a social being, related to others. In the light of these three elements, Israel, the people of God, discovers its purpose in life: *man exists to move together with "the others" and with the whole of creation towards a final fulfillment in God.* He is not a victim as in the interpretation of other civilizations. His solidarity with others is not the product of the wrathful gods from whom he has to seek defense by sticking together with others. Man in the Bible has become aware that it is God himself who wants and even orders the humans to love one another. Finally, the universe is not against him, as people in other civilizations frustrating declare. The man of God in the Bible firmly believes that he is growing with the universe, almost like its most creative force, even cooperating with God in its completion. And God, who is most powerful, not like Mardouk or Zeus, has given a meaning and a purpose to the universe: the promise of life.

Man's purpose in life in the Old Testament is astonishingly similar to the purpose in life man keeps discovering thousands of years later. Despite human selfishness, narrow mindedness, and confusion, this purpose in life always makes sense and seems to grow in everyman's heart almost like a spiritual instinct.

The Old Testament becomes more than a historical document. Israel's growing awareness recorded in the Bible can be translated into a way of living, a true spirituality. The guidelines and general direction about morality, in the broad sense, of how to go about life, becomes *universal and transcultural* in the mature period of Israel.

The Old Testament today aids us as a manual, enabling us to discover our purpose in life, our rights and duties, serving as the basis for an ethical direction and even the way to understand ourselves when we contradict these ethical principles, either out of weakness or by misusing our freedom. The Old Testament helps us to understand the two contradictory forces that seem to pull us apart either to destruction or to union in love with one another and the universe. The Old Testament clearly affirms the realistic and positive attitude of man in the universe: hope. There is always a positive balance at the end. Man is destined to salvation. Life is hopeful!

This view of life is corroborated by man's experience in history. If hope has not been present in the human beings, they would never have been able to progress. If hope was not present in the world today, through its confusing and unstable reality, there would not be any future. Life would come to a stop. Maybe hope is part of man's collective unconscious and to live in hope is intrinsic to our desire for transcendence.

The people of Israel in their mature period try to interpret and to give an answer to the fundamental questions of life, the purpose of our existence. Israel then suggests the ideal of love as the universal force. This mysterious force, contradictory to our on selfishness, seems to be the inner force that moves inside of us, personally and socially. This is the force, explained by Teilhard de Chardin, which moves the universal cosmic evolution.

This is when Israel comes up with the almost incomprehensible twist of the Suffering Servant of Isaiah. Only with the universal openness of his maturity could he interpret love as self-sacrifice with an infinite and universal redeeming value. Only at the peak of his self-understanding, his social acceptance of others, and the deep awareness of his spiritual transcendence, could man understand the deepest meaning of love.

This meaning acquires universal proportions in the figure of Christ. He is the turning point of man's history. In Christ man becomes aware of the true and profound purpose of life.

## CONCLUSION PART II

We have chosen the Judeo-Christian tradition to find an answer to our deepest question of our purpose in life. We have followed the historical reflections of a people that brought us a new vision of life. This positive vision inspires our pursuit of happiness.

The Judeo-Christian tradition develops around the idea of man discovering his identity, society, and the universe that surrounds him. From the primitive nomad man, in Abraham, to the sophisticated thinker in the mature period of Israel, human thought expands. This development is a true anthropological experience with a universal value for all times, especially for all who are seriously looking for happiness.

The growth of the Judeo-Christian culture follows a distinct and extraordinary direction with other ancient cultures. Despite its profoundly realistic out look, the Judeo-Christian tradition, unlike others, is positively directed to life and to a hopeful view of man, his world, and the universe.

This understanding of life is not, by any means, just an explanation of the past, as in many histories of other civilizations, but also a vision of the future. The Bible has an open ending, or even more exactly, no ending at all. It can be considered an explanation of the first cycle in history, the pattern which the present and the future cycles in history follow. The biblical vision interprets life in general and the process of the universe toward the future.

Israel has followed the same life process as any individual. Israel has lived and grown through the same three stages of life: Centration, Decentration, and Super-centration. As the people of Israel grow from childhood, in the patriarchs, through adolescence in the desert and under the kings, into maturity with the prophets and sages, they discover their purpose in life. They become aware of the *principle and foundation* of all existence: a God who is the creator and who gives direction and purpose to all creation. The people of Israel that they are invited to cooperate freely in the completion and fulfillment of that creation. They have a special call, an invitation, from that God who is a loving friend, protector, challenger, always present in a transcendental promise. This living God is involved in history and does care for justice and for truth in his creation.

Through their process of maturation the people of Israel discover a way of acting upon, or better, responding to, that relationship with God and his creation. Through their groping, their mistakes, and their reflection upon their experiences, the people of Israel have recorded in the Bible some basic attitudes and main directions of life. These constitute a way of living, a true spirituality that transcends the Hebrew or the Jewish mentality and becomes truly universal and transcultural. As the people of Israel become mature, they discover their true solidarity with all humankind. They have found answers for all humanity.

The message of the Old Testament is that *man's purpose in life is life itself.* All mankind is called to life and to hope for life. Through vicissitudes, struggles, and death man is promised life in a higher and deeper dimensions.

In the singular sense, this life may be called *self-realization* or self-transcendence. In the collective sense, to use the biblical concept, this life may be called *salvation*. Mankind, in general, is called to salvation through different stages of life. These stages grow outwardly from the individual through the social toward the universal. At the same time, the outward growth produces an inward awareness of higher and deeper dimensions in man himself. This process of deeper humanization or *hominization*, as Teilhard de Chardin has called it, produces in man a deeper consciousness and a more sensitive integration with reality. Life is a process of continuous spiritual integration. In no way do persons disappear in others and in the universe, on the contrary, persons become more persons and increasingly fulfilled.

The Old Testament, however, emphasizes human success and hope in temporal "glory" as the ideal of life, at least until the appearance of the Suffering Servant in Isaiah's writings. The figure of the Messiah announced as a not humanly successful suffering man brings an unexpected twist to history and human logic. Christ comes as a paradox to the Jewish tradition, making everyone think more deeply. There comes a new scandal which will produce a schism in Hebrew thinking. They will not accept this suffering Messiah so long announced and desired. *"He came to his own and his own people did not accept him"* (John 1: 11). They would not accept the new dimension.

As we have said, the Suffering Servant of Yahweh, identified in Christ, the Star of David, the Promise, comes to announce to us a new dimension. This is something as profound and mysterious as life itself. God chooses the highest expression to show his love: the love of self-giving in sacrifice. This love possesses a redeeming and liberating power which transcends all reason.

The world keeps enticing us with easy and superficial answers. We are constantly charmed by selfish and false expressions of love. These eventually enslave and destroy us. Only with this kind of humble self giving, can man find true freedom, fulfillment and happiness.

---

*After studying the promise of salvation as expressed in the history of the people of Israel, let us discover a very intriguing New Testament. Let us find how that promise announced for centuries became a reality in a figure that has transcended history, cultures, and time: Jesus of Nazareth, the so called Christ.*

# PART III

# A NEW VISION FOR THE PURPOSE OF LIFE

## (16) IN THE FULLNESS OF TIME

*Christianity enters history through the Roman Empire*

Historians commonly agree that the Roman Empire was the most advanced structure of imperial government the world has ever known. The Roman ruins, all over the Europe, the near East, and the Middle East, still speak of an extraordinary, creative fusion of elements unmatched in history. Bridges, roads, aqueducts, theatres, temples, and other monuments tell us the story of the Roman Empire during the 350 years when at the height of their unparalleled power, they had their greatest impact on the world.

"The Roman Empire produced a definite consciousness of world history, in contrast to accidental national histories," declares Paul Tillich. The universalism of the Roman Empire meant something negative and positive at the same time. Negatively it meant the breakdown of national religions and cultures. Positively it meant the idea of mankind as a whole could be conceived at that time. With all their drawbacks the Romans certainly created the idea of a universal community in their territories. Politics involved the true content of the world. Not only the aristocracy, but also the rural communities, the people in their colonies, and even the slaves influenced the destiny of the Empire. All the roads led to Rome… Along these roads came Cleopatra with all the Egyptian background of centuries. Through these roads the Romans conquered and colonized all the countries that encircled the Mediterranean. They brought their "booty" back home through the same roads. In this booty they brought to Rome the Greek thought which the Romans always admired and worshiped. Hellenistic thinking permeated and even shaped the Roman culture, its philosophy, its religion, its literature, and the plastic arts.

By the same roads came thousands of immigrants and slaves from all the countries conquered by the Roman legions. The slaves literally built and made functioned the city and the empire that ruled the world for many centuries. With their different backgrounds these foreigners contributed to the cosmopolitan character of Rome. By one of those roads came some Jewish immigrants from a poor colony east of the Mediterranean. Peter and Paul walked into Rome at the peak of the Roman times carrying with them a strange message from some controversial man who had just been executed on a cross in Jerusalem as a criminal, Jesus of Nazareth. "According to the Apostle Paul," says Tillich, "there does not always exist the possibility that, that can happen which, for example, happened in the appearance of Jesus the Christ. This happened in one special moment in history when everything was ready for it to happen. Paul speaks of the 'kairos' in describing the feeling that the time was ripe, matured of prepared.

*God has given us the wisdom to understand fully the mystery, the plan he was pleased to decree in Christ, to be carried out in the fullness of time: namely to bring all things in the heavens and on earth into one under Christ's headship.*
Eph. 1: 9- 10

In the fullness of time, in Rome, a new faith appeared as a mere whisper that grew louder and louder later on with the joyful chants of the dying Christians in the circus. History scholar Michael Grant declares: "for no faith could parallel the simple, complete assertion that, in fulfilment of the Hebrew Scriptures which were now widely available in Greek translations, Jesus died to save mankind. This suffering –of life given to man originally, lost by man, and restored to him by Redemption—was a concept unknown to the pagan mysteries. And their 'eternal life' promise lacked the vivid urgency of the higher, more divine, and more glorious destiny, the very life of God himself, which was promised to the Christian believer. The Saviour, too, was no subordinate deity, no created being endowed with human shape as intermediary between God and man, but God himself incarnate."

But the real strength of Christianity, continues Grant, the truly unique and exciting feature which in the end caused it to outstrip all other religions, was its founder's message of love –profoundly original in its emphasis despite all that it had selected from earlier Rabbinical teachings. This was a doctrine of total, revolutionary, unrestricted love, charity, and sympathy—not excluding woman, since Jesus was born of a human woman; extended to the children; embracing even the totally hopeless and destitute, those whom society had rejected, as it rejected and humiliated the weakness upon earth of Jesus himself; and uncompromisingly proclaimed by a Son of God who had truly and recently lived among mankind, and whose promise of immortality was firmly based upon love.

The teachings attributed to Jesus, for all their detailed affinities with Hebrew thought, made a vivid new appeal. The Greco-Roman philosophies and religions had stimulated the imaginative faculty in religious thought, had supplied the longings, have quickened man's faith and sometimes also their sense of purity. But they had not presented so gloriously definite a promise of immortality. For the Christians, this promise was concrete indeed, actually compromising a bodily resurrection; and no one was too wretched to be excluded from it. By their universal extension of the *mystery* the Christians soared beyond their pagan contemporaries. The excitement of uniting under such love (for all humanity), and attempting to repay it, made them ready to bring death willingly upon their faith for the sake of their faith. So they convincingly sang with joy when thrown to the lions.

The Christian idea came with extraordinary simplicity, communicated by a group of uneducated but down-to-earth men and women of deep conviction. Nevertheless, the Christian message carried a richness and depth that shocked the Roman thinking. Maybe these apostles of Christianity never realized the revolutionary impact they were having in history.

Christianity appeared in a world strongly influenced by Greek philosophy. The Christian philosophy had to face and confront the elaborated and sophisticated Greek understanding of God.

Both in Greek philosophy and Jewish symbolism the *Logos* is the cosmic principle of creation. The concept *Logos* was adequate in so far as it expressed the universal manifestation of God in all forms of reality. Yet the Logos is an abstract universal principle, whereas Jesus is a concrete reality. Christianity brings this great paradox to the

Greco-Roman world of its time: *the logos became flesh*. Tillich declares: "The idea that the universal Logos became flesh could never have been derived from the Greek thought... The greatness of the New Testament is that it was able to use words, concepts, and symbols which had developed in the history of religions and at the same time preserved the picture of Jesus who was interpreted by them. The spiritual power of the New Testament was great enough to take all these concepts into Christianity, with all their pagan and Jewish connotations, without losing the basic reality, namely, the event of Jesus as the Christ, which these concepts were supposed to interpret."

There are two key figures in the "inculturation" process of the Christian message into the Greco-Roman world. The first is Paul of Tarsus, persecutor of the early Christians converted on the road to Damascus. He is a Jewish scribe and a pharisee, and an intellectual. He became the apostle of the gentiles and with surprising open mindedness went over the other apostles, inclusive Peter. These maintained that the message of Christ should only be received through Judaism, that is, the gentiles could be baptized by accepting Judaism first.

Paul, the pharisee studious of the Jewish Law, who could have been the intransigent and stuck to the Jewish tradition, was the one who directly brought Christianity to the Greco-Roman world.

At the Acropolis in Athens we can still see the place where Paul stood to speak about their "unknown God." Paul's letters to the different Christian communities he organized, were the first written documents of Christianity, just a few years after Christ's death and resurrection. In these letters it appears the same Christian attitude that later on was explained in the gospels as Christ's message. These are the first accounts on the Eucharist, the resurrection of Christ, and the first written testimony that Christ was the Son of God.

Paul's preaching was not an easy task that brought instant conversion to his listeners. Complaining but convincingly he declares: "For Jews demand signs and Greeks look for wisdom, but we proclaim Christ crucified a stumbling block for the Jews and foolishness to Gentiles, but to those who are called, Jews and Greeks alike, Christ the power of God and the wisdom of God." (1 Corinthians 1: 18)

The second most important figure in the merging of Christianity with the Greco-Roman thinking was John the evangelist, who in his old age wrote the fourth gospel in the Greek language from Greece itself where he lived in exile. He uses the concept "Logos" emphasizing on his Christian assertion that the "Logos" became flesh and lived among us. With that beginning of his gospel, John reconciles the Greek thinking with a concept that, as we said before, could have never derived from the Greek: Jesus the Christ was the "Logos," the eternal and incomprehensible God who became man to save all humanity.

Paul and John were decisive figures to the unique sociological phenomenon of a small insignificant sect from a remote Roman colony would become the world religion which united the East and the West. Judaism, despite its belief in one universal God that also included the gentiles, could have never become into a universal religion for all humanity. Only Christianity has ever been close to the ideal of establishing a universal community based in serving one another in love – the ideal that conquered the Roman world.

The Jewish-Christian apostles were not announcing, however, a new sect or philosophical ideology and definitely not a new "religion." They claimed to be announcing, right then, in the fullness of time, something that has been happening since the beginning of time. Paul is saying that actually there is a universal revelatory power going through all history and preparing for that which Christianity considers to be the ultimate revelation. This ultimate revelation, as he sees it, is centred in the figure of Jesus the Christ.

The first Christian communities developed around this idea. They were composed by apostles, prophets, teachers, men and women with different talents and functions. The Christian communities, or churches, were founded by Paul in the image of a "body" where all the parts were important. These parts would function as *diakonia*, that is, a real loving service between the different parts of that "body" in humble interaction.

Later on, bishops and presbyters appeared, not so much as authority figures, but as always oriented to serve and guide these communities. Christ's words about the ideal to be of service to others were clearly and practically understood. Thus, it appeared the concept *ecclesia*, the community called Church.

What appealed many from the beginning was the solidarity with the poor and the suffering. Also, the cohesiveness of the early Christians, attracted many followers. Their liturgical expressions to worship God included men and women, without any distinctions of race, social classes, or level of education. Together they shared the Eucharist, peak of their liturgical expression. They shared all their goods and riches, not by obligation or imposition, but in a true and sincere reciprocal love. The ones who had more helped the one who had less.

Historian Henry Chadwick calls this phenomenon "the Christian paradox."

This was the most peaceful revolution ever recorded in history, and it extended through all the territories of the Roman Empire. It was also a phenomenon growing from the low strata of society without any conscious ideological or political connotation. This ideal conquered a contrasting Roman society openly based on power, hedonistic and materialistic practices. Christian spirituality would seem to ridicule the old traditional forms of bloody sacrifices, incense, temples and statues of the Roman and Greek gods. This new ideal began slowly to attract the intellectual and wealthy classes, and eventually figures of the imperial court and Roman army officers. Christianity was really a revolution in the history of humanity.

During the first years of Christianity, under the persecutions that succeeded one another, the first communities lived with the intense piety and passion of a new-found faith. The first so called fathers or doctors of the church, to defend this new way of thinking, concentrated all their efforts to present Christianity to the Greco-Roman world in its own terms. They wrote in Greek and in Latin, using Hellenistic terms with the understandable philosophical forms and concepts of the time. This was the sophisticated peak of Greek expression now adopted by the Roman Empire.

The Christian forefathers intelligently applied Plato's metaphysical theories. They even proclaimed philosophers like Heraclitus and Socrates as "Christians before Christ."

Christianity was presented as the true philosophy. John the evangelist had already made his point by bringing the concept *Logos*, the Word or eternal expression implanted in each human being, as the "seed of truth." This had enlightened, not only the prophets of Israel, but also the Greek sages, and finally had taken human form in Jesus the Christ.

Among these Fathers of the Church, was Origen of Alexandria, who invented theology as a science, struggled for a definitive reconciliation between Christianity and the Greek world. Thus, Christianity was presented as the most perfect of all religions. The image of God, darkened by man's sin and guilt, would return and restored in Christ. God's "enfleshment" would lead towards divinization of all human beings.

Nevertheless, this thinking shifted the original emphasis of Christianity, centred in the cross and resurrection of Christ, into the pre-existence of the *Logos* and the Son of God, took its toll in the historical Christian message. We are well aware of the negative effects of this Hellenistic interpretation. In its Hebrew origins Christianity was not only theory, but *practice*: an attitude of life. Greek thinking, in contrast, stressed the accepting truth and the mystery of Jesus, and not so much the imitation of Christ in his attitudes and teachings.

---

*This brief study on how Christianity came to enter into the Greco-Roman world is of vital importance to step into the mysterious figure of Jesus the Christ. Although following the same unique and unprecedented positive vision of life developed by the people of Israel, Jesus seems to bring us a new message. Christ's message of salvation and the promise of happiness surpassed its own originality. It brings also a new sense of urgency in the responsibility to announce this to all nations.*

*Let us follow with curiosity and willingness this direction which is promising us the universally desired happiness we are searching.*

---

## 17) AN ENIGMATIC UNIQUE FIGURE IN HISTORY
*Who is this Jesus Christ?*

The figure of Christ has been studied and interpreted through many different approaches: the cosmological, the anthropological, and the historical. The oldest but constantly recurrent approach sees belief in Christ from a cosmological perspective. This approach has been renewed in the XX century by Teilhard de Chardin who sees Jesus Christ as the *evolution* fully (self-) realized. We can see now, more than ever, how important it is to take in consideration all those different approaches instead of isolating each aspect separately. The historical reality, the universal answer, and the saving power bring us together a complete vision of Christ's total reality. This third way of presenting –a saving power-- combines the two others in a higher unity. The foregoing shows that the person and history of Jesus are inseparable from their universal significance; and equally, that the significance of Jesus is inseparable from his person and history.

Anthropologically, we have been given the explanation, the growing story of a revelation as it was understood by the Jewish people throughout their history. We have followed the line of progress, or evolution, discovered by them, recorded in the Old Testament of the Bible. The signs, the prophecies, and announcements all converge on the figure of Christ as the realization of *the promise*. The anthropological approach has led us in a concurrence of lines to that focal point in history: the figure of Christ. Walter Kasper declares that anthropology is the grammar which God uses to express himself. Yet, the meaning, the electricity which gives life to all that anatomical "description" needs the contribution of faith. Ultimately the mystery of Christ can be accepted only by faith.

The gospels present evidence about Jesus in the form of a narrative. They are intended as witnesses to faith in the earthly and risen Jesus. The narrative on the life of Jesus is understood in the light of faith. Kasper declares that an understanding of this point does not justify any exaggerated scepticism about historical basis of the New Testament narrative, but it does rule out any uncritical, pseudo-biblical fundamentalism.

For example, the infancy narratives (in midrashic style) or stories of Jesus' childhood in Matthew and Luke offer very little material for tracing the course of his life. They describe Jesus' early life on Old Testament models, especially by analogy with the story of Moses. Their concern is more theological than biographical; their purpose is to say: "Jesus is the fulfilment of the Old Testament." We are on slightly firmer historical grounds, Kasper continues, in regard to the beginning and the end of Jesus' public life, which began with John's baptism of Jesus in the Jordan and ended with the death on the cross in Jerusalem.

Even if we did not receive the history of the Jewish people, recorded in the Old Testament, which had slowly led us to find the promise of Christ, the figure of Jesus arrives with an overwhelming force. Jesus Christ, no doubt, has been the most the most fascinating and controversial figure of all times.

In our search for happiness, we are intrigued by how Jesus with his two-thousand year old message is still a recurrent theme in all parts of the world, all cultures and races in their different social classes.

Ultimately, however, Jesus fits into no categories; he is the man who destroys all categories. He is different from John the Baptist. Jesus does not lead a life of withdrawn asceticism apart from the world. He approaches people and lives among them. He wants nothing for himself, but everything for God and others. He does not belong to the establishment, but comes from humble origins and retains a feeling for the everyday distress and troubles of the poor. His respect for women is striking in a man of the ancient world. He does not look on poverty and disease as punishments from God; the poor and sick are particular objects of God's love. He goes after the lost, the lost sheep, the lost coin, the prodigal son... Most striking of all, even at the time, was that he brought even sinners and misfits, the ritually impure and the outcasts into his company. He even invites them to eat with him. But there is no sign of hatred or envy of the rich. He gets along even with exploiters, the tax collectors; he summons one or two of them, like Matthew, into the immediate circle of his disciples. Class-war slogans find no direct support in Jesus. His fight is not against political authorities, but against the daemonic powers of evil manifested in personal or social selfishness or sin.

Jesus has no program. There is nothing planned or organized about his career. He does the will of God as he recognizes here and now. It is in prayer to the father, his father, that he has his deepest roots. The final end of his service to others is that men should recognize the goodness of God and praise him. He is not just the man for others, but the man from God and for God. Jesus is not a trained theologian. He speaks simply, vividly and directly. Ordinary people very soon see the difference between Jesus and theological experts and lawyers. Jesus teaches with authority (Mk 1: 22-27). His disciples regarded him as a prophet. This was the common judgement of him. And he placed himself in the line of the prophets to stir, awake, and promote consciousness. But if he claims to be more than Jonah, more than Solomon, who was this man who so lightly set himself to be above John the Baptist, whom he called was more than a prophet?

This "more" has an eschatological ring. Jesus is not just one in the line of prophets, but the eschatological one: the last, the definitive, all-transcending prophet. He is filled with the Spirit of God (Mk 3:28-29). In contemporary Jewish thinking, declares Walter Kasper, the Spirit of God had died out after the time of the prophets. God is silent. Not until the last times is the Spirit expected again. When Jesus is seen as a charismatic and a prophet of the last times, that means that the time has come. The painful period of God's absence is over. God has broken his silence. He let his voice be heard again. He performs works of power among his people. The time of grace has dawned. But it was a very offputting dawn—quite different from what had been generally expected. Could a handful of uneducated and quite dubious people, asks Kasper reflectively, be the turning-point of world history?

These disciples were announcing to the whole world a man who claimed to be the Son of God. This Son of God claimed to be sent to the world with the mission of announcing the kingdom of love of a God who had revealed himself in history as a loving father of all human beings.

Kasper, in his book, *Jesus the Christ*, asserts that Jesus does not fit into any category. Neither ancient nor modern, nor Old Testament categories are adequate to understand him. He is unique. He is and remains a mystery. He himself does little to illuminate this mystery. He is not interested in himself at all. He is interested in only one thing, but interested in it totally: God's coming rule in love. He is interested in God and human beings, in God's history with human beings. That is his mission. We get closer to the mystery of his person when we look into that mission.

Nevertheless, Jesus was a normal person, declares José Luis Martín Descalzo. But if we define "normal" in the sense of the narrow indedness and selfishness that affects most of the human race, and makes human irresponsible, Jesus, obviously was not a normal man. Jesus knew what he wanted. His words were clear and transparent, presenting always basic realities in a manner which at once enlightened and challenged, as Romano Guardini used to say. Jesus' parables invited to think, always with an unexpected twist that made us ponder and reflect. His words were like an arrow snapped towards action.

It is sad to see the many Christian leaders who seem to forget Christ's teachings and attitude beautifully described in the gospels. Many resort to just stress obedience to the authority and the rules just as the pharisees did in times of Christ.

Martín Descalzo declares that Jesus did not disclose any new big revelations, neither did he tried to attract attention by disconcerting ideas and novelties. He says reasonable things which helped people face life. His observations are more out of common sense than high philosophical elaborations.

It is also surprising Jesus' tremendous freedom in his teachings to the disciples. Never before has a founder left such a non-institutionalized vast and free task. He did not leave the apostles any of the structures that followed in the history of the Church, unless it was the celebration of reunions from time to time to celebrate a supper in his memory and his future coming. Everything else was left open in the hands of this expected Paraclete, the Holy Spirit, who will teach them everything and remember them all what he has said. (John 14: 26)

Christ cannot definitely be praised as a great philosopher or even a great man like many agnostics praise him. He was either completely crazy, or he was truly the Son of God. No man has ever claimed to be the Son of God as he had, his disciples gave their lives for it, and his enemies, the Hebrew priests and lawyers, killed him for that reason. Christ forgave, in his own name, the sins of the people, an intolerable blasphemy in the Jewish tradition. Only God could forgive sins!

Many of the gospel readings show that Christ presented himself as much more than a man: as the plenitude of man, someone equal to his Father, God himself in person. Without accepting these affirmations, Martin Descalzo says, nothing else can be accepted of the gospels. Jesus acts and talks like someone who has power over nature, over the law, over sin, salvation and condemnation. His disciples, even though they were never able to understand all this while he was alive, will confess it openly in every page of the New Testament and sealed it with their own lives.

Yet this answer is purely provisory. Jesus, says Martín Descalzo, must be judged by his fruits all along his life.

---

*Let us agree with Martin Descalzo in continuing looking for a deeper and more complete answer about Jesus of Nazareth. Even though we have already found this key personage in our pursuit of happiness, we must continue to find and study his true message. We must find out if Jesus really has an answer for our question about happiness.*

---

## 18) THE MESSAGE FROM A KINGDOM OUT OF THIS WORLD.
*A kingdom not of this world, yet already present in this world.*

Jesus had something to say; he delivered a definite and concrete message.

The "good news," according to the gospels, comes as a change of attitude, a new awareness of life: the true purpose in life. Marks sums up the content of Jesus message thus: *"The time is fulfilled, and the Kingdom of God is at hand; repent and believe in the Gospel* (Mk 1: 15)

This calling of Jesus, in the social context of the time, must have sound like a bell awakening the hearts of all who heard it, Martin Descalzo writes dramatically. It did not invite either to revolt or to kill, however, it was certainly most radical and revolutionary. What it meant was the coming of a new era, the changing the very roots and foundations of the whole world. The Christ was ready to respond those questions always puzzling the human mind. He had answers to define the purpose of life and furthermore to give sense to death and suffering. Why does man want peace and still nourishes himself with hatred? Why do some oppress others, and the others strive to turn things around and become themselves in oppressors? Why do men yearn for God, and when they find him, leave him and forget him? Why does loneliness devour our soul?

And here it is, when nobody was expecting it, someone arrives with answers, announces a new and different world and invites all to the fascinating adventure of receiving the message and built this new world.

Someone who does not bring theoretical answers, but who is willing to be the first adventurer and leader: who himself embodies this announced kingdom.

At first, Christ's contemporaries must have been astonished. Then intrigued by these new ideas, they were finally overwhelmed with an enormous enthusiasm. At last something different had happened! What everybody had dreamed without daring to think about! A cry of liberation came from within that is still valid and alive for all humanity. Mark had announced it: the Kingdom of God is at hand, change your ways and believe the good news! The framework of Jesus' preaching and mission was the approaching Kingdom of God.

This kingdom means a transformation of all human beings towards a new dimension. Jesus does not come to better the human being, he comes to create a *new* human being altogether! Jesus is preaching something completely revolutionary which includes our inner being as well as the external, the spiritual as well as the mundane, the individual and the community, this world and the other... Jesus is asking us to direct our lives into a different direction. Surprisingly he tells us that this kingdom is already here, it has begun in a process of time, like a seed that must germinate and eventually grow. This process involves both the individual and the community. According to Jesus' preaching his kingdom is inside of us, not enclosed but open to all reality. It is definitely germinating in the hearts of all who could listen.

Jesus is announcing liberation from all evil, ignorance, and selfishness. His kingdom will transform a universe ruled by ambitious power, money, and selfish pleasure, into anew kingdom ruled by love, service of others, and true freedom.

Nevertheless, human beings will keep with their heresies of yesterday and today. They will try to diminish God's work and "boxing" it into small exclusive categories either on the social, or just the political, or the psychologically personal. They will go from one extreme to the other never trying to understand the full meaning of Christ's message. The Kingdom of God announced by Jesus implies much more than these particular changes. It means a radical transformation in the relationships of all human beings in which mutual service would substitute selfishness and manipulative dominion of one another. It means a real change in which humans would respect the lives of all others. It would be a change or heart in which love would not be enslaved by selfish and irresponsible sexual pleasure. In this kingdom true freedom would rule internally and externally. The idols created by narrow human minds would be toppled and the God of life and salvation will reign in each individual and in the human universal society.

Mysteriously, this God respects human freedom, so the kingdom must develop through a long growing process, individually, socially, and universally. According to the historical process taught by the Jewish people, the Kingdom of God must occurred by an evolution in time. The Kingdom of God is already at hand, it is a reality, however, it must keep growing through a dynamic evolution in which all human beings, all of us, are invited to participate and to complete it.

## 19) A UNIVERSAL ANSWER?

*Can Jesus answer all the fundamental questions of man?*

Even though Jesus nowhere tells his contemporary Jewish hearers in so many words what the Kingdom of God is, he presupposes in them a familiarity with that idea of the Kingdom. Is this Kingdom of God the realization of the promise given to Abraham and confirmed and announced throughout the history of Israel? Is Christ himself, his mystery, his message, the Kingdom of God?

Christ speaks of freedom, justice and forgiveness. He criticizes hypocrisy, stagnation, and judgemental attitudes. Jesus seems to be speaking of a new dimension, maybe a new way to understand the Covenant or even the possibility of a totally new "pact" between God and man. The signs become clearer in the light of the Old Testament tradition. Isaiah has announced the Messiah as the Suffering Servant.

Two centuries have passed since Isaiah described him. Jesus presents himself as the one whom the patriarchs waited for and whose day they longed to see. *"Your father Abraham rejoiced that he might see my day. He saw it and was glad."* (John 8: 56)

Simeon, the holy old man in the temple who was waiting to see the consolation of Israel, held the child Jesus in his arms and praised the Lord:

> *Now, Master, you can dismiss*
> *your servant in peace;*
> *for you have fulfilled your word.*
> *For my eyes have witnessed your saving deed*
> *displayed for all the people to see*
> *a revealing light to the gentiles,*
> *and glory of your people Israel.* (Lk. 29- 32)

To the question posed by John the Baptist's disciples if he was the One who must come, Jesus answers: *"Go back and report to John what you hear and see: the blind recover their sight, cripples walk, lepers are cured, the deaf hears, dead men are raised to life, and the poor have the good news preached to them. Blest is the man who finds no stumbling block in me."* (Mt 11: 4- 6)

Christ, according to his witnesses, is the realization of the promise. Paul says of him:

*"He is the image of the invisible God, the first born of all creatures. In him everything in heaven and on earth was created, things visible and invisible, whether thrones and dominations, principalities or powers. In him everything continues in being".* (Col 1: 15- 17)

John the evangelist refers to Christ as the *word*, the *Logos* become flesh. This Greek interpretation gives to the Jewish promise a universal character. Christ is the realization of a universal promise of salvation.

*The word became flesh
and made his dwelling among us,
and we have seen his glory:
the glory of an only Son coming from the Father,
filled with enduring love.* (John 1: 14)

It is John, the Evangelist, who identifies Christ with the Suffering Servant of Isaiah. As he gives the testimony of the Baptist just before the baptism of Jesus, the announcement is made: *"Look! There is the lamb of God who takes away the sin of the world!"* (John 1: 29)

The covenant is the pivotal point in the history of Israel. The Jewish people consider this unique event evidence of their unity as a nation and people. By the covenant they boldly express their distinction of being considered the "chosen people." The whole Old Testament is written in the light of the covenant as its most important event.

The covenant between God and man has been established first in Abraham to express the loving personal relationship between God and creation. God makes a pact with Abraham and asks Abraham to seal it with blood. With the circumcision of his foreskin everyman will actively seal the pact with God. Abraham is blessed with an eternal blessing and through him all children of Israel. At Mount Sinai Moses renews the pact with God in the name of his people. The covenant then becomes, with the law, a written statement for posterity. Nevertheless, Christ seems to be talking now of a *new and everlasting covenant* in which all mankind will be blessed forever. This new covenant, as he seems to emphasize, is a unique feature of the new law, the center for Christianity and history of all humankind.

Matthew and Mark both stress the importance of this new pact between God and man with its new characteristics. In their Gospels they try to convey the depth and meaning of the mystery. Matthew's narrative of the Sermon on the Mount views with a sensitive understanding the solemnity of the occasion. Matthew and Mark recorded this new covenant, setting the scene upon the mountain (evidently a well known symbol in evangelical tradition). Matthew sees in Jesus the new Moses who promulgated the new Covenant on a new Sinai.

Jesus, seeing the crowds, went up the mountain. He sat down with his disciples. Then he began teaching:

*How blessed are the poor in spirit: the reign of God is theirs*

In the world of ancient Rome where Christianity made its first appearance, these words must have sounded absurd, as these might be today. To preach poverty in a world in which everybody wants to be rich, seems contradictory in the search for happiness. Decadent Rome and our society today, both, praise richness, excessive luxuries, success, power, selfish pleasure, and possession of all unimaginable "things." This hunger for riches goes to such exorbitant levels, that even the poor are willing to sacrifice everything to pursuit something that never makes happy even the most rich and famous. Hundreds of thousands emigrate from their poor countries to the cities of developed countries looking for a so called paradise that does not exist. They are immediately enslaved, not only by these dehumanizing systems in which only money counts, but also by their own instincts an their own unquenchable thirst for economic goods. Soon after they arrived to their "new world," they become obsessive compulsive consumerists. They want to possess all what the media assures them to make them instantly happy, just like the rich…

Nobody wants poverty, still poor countries are becoming increasingly poor. The poor and the marginalized in our developed countries grow more and more frustrated as they cannot "compete" with the rich. In the big cities crime and delinquency keep escalating maybe because the frustrated ones unscrupulously try to become rich at all costs. On the other hand, the rich, especially those who have built an "easy and quick" fortune, try to ignore the poor and stuff their eyes and ears with more extravagant forms of luxury. The sad result is that everybody seems to be unhappy and live in constant anguish.

And Christ opens his sermon on the mount with this seemingly outrageous blessing of the poor. However, it seems clear he is not referring to simple economic poverty, he speaks in a higher level with a depth that makes us reflect and ponder. Jesus states clearly that happiness is not related to have possessions, or to dominate with power, or to be humanly successful and enjoy deceitful pleasure, but in truly loving others and being loved. This seems like a paradox in worldly terms, most especially in today's world.

Jesus is not praising the lack of material riches. He is definitely going beyond the problem of money. A person can be materially poor and have nothing, yet have a monstrous materialistic ambition which usually degenerates in selfish envy and bitter resentment against the "rich" and everybody else. They usually are potential oppressors who, when they get some riches and power, despise and denigrate their own. This is certainly not the poverty blessed by Christ.

On the other hand, Christ could not condone the irresponsible materially rich, some of whom would use the excuse of not being attached to their riches. Christ does not condone those who live idly comfortably doing nothing for others, and of course, not trying to change unjust social, economic, and political structures, from which they irresponsibly profit.

Christ had already talked about the riches that oppress and kill, in contrast to the true riches that give life to others and give fruit socially and universally.

Christ seems to refer to a poverty of spirit that means *a liberation which includes love.* This liberation invites to humility and simplicity, without extravagant luxury.

This spiritual poverty Christ is blessing, seems to be an ideal utopia almost impossible to obtain. Then, who could possibly be saved? The disciples, intrigued, ask Jesus after they hear the passage of the camel through the eye of a needle... Christ answers: *"To men this is impossible to understand, but to God everything is possible."* (Mt 19: 24- 25)

God's mercy goes beyond the human imagination. However, one way or another, God helps us to encounter our own poverty, maybe through infirmity, difficult hopeless situations, human failure, or even some mysterious emotional or physical crisis, which surely would awake us from our complacent lethargy. There are many ways in which we feel forced to look up and find God in our necessity and limitations. Only through our own poverty, when we feel dependent on others, finally in need, we are able to understand true riches.

Just by humbly accepting our own poverty, our needy human condition, our thirst for happiness, we can understand Christ astonishing blessing: Blessed, happy, are those who are poor in spirit, the Reign of God is theirs!

But woe to those who keep thinking they could buy happiness with "placebos" and wasteful entertainment while stepping on others! Woe to those who try to ignore their own needs and the needs of others, by not thinking and reflecting! Woe to those who numb themselves against their call to be responsible.

Still, this first beatitude opens a new dimension in the pursuit of happiness. How blessed, how happy are the poor in spirit, the reign of God, true richness and creative power, is theirs!

*Blessed are the sorrowing, they shall be consoled.*

And right there, we all should be included, all humanity, in this blessing, because, everywhere, just by being human and "exposed" to life, all of us suffer and cry. We cry because we feel vulnerable to all elements and the evil surrounding us. We cry when we suffer injustice and feel our helplessness. We sorrow in our loneliness and dark despair. The mother cries when her child is hungry or is sick. She lives in sorrow watching him breathe and pant in deep suffering. We all grieve when a loved one dies or leaves us. We also cry when we empathy in solidarity with the pain and suffering of others. Our history keeps reminding us the tragedies and catastrophes. War and massacres keep recurring helping us to be sensitive and solidary. We feel desperately hopeless in trying to prevent them.

And we cry in a deep and abysmal pain that only God is capable to console.

Blessed are those who sorrow, they will be consoled, and definitely promised to be consoled by God himself!

*Blessed are the lowly; they shall inherit the land.*

Patience is perhaps the most important virtue, and yet the most underestimated. This beatitude is often translated as: "Blessed are the meek and humble of heart." And there it is: the best definition for those who are patient. Jesus tells us: *"Learn from me, for I am gentle and humble of heart."* (Mt: 11: 29) Here we go back to centuries of Christianity inviting us to imitate Christ in his attitude and teachings. To be meek, gentle, and humble of heart, does not mean being weak and not strong. It definitely means to show gently one's inner strength. In other words, it means to be patient. Patience shows the acceptance of others as they are, with love and forgiveness, however, with sufficient strength to help change difficult and challenging situations. Then, the patient one, gentle and meek, would always be an agent of reconciliation. In front of matrimonial or family crises between brothers or friends, this beatitude must make us reflect on what it means to be gentle and humble of heart: to be meek and strongly patient.

Thus, to help solve critical situations in social, political, or economical conflicts, this beatitude will help understand the true meaning of its "prize" and blessing from Christ: they will inherit the land. The Kingdom of God is already here, but it must keep growing and developing in time by the strong commitment and patient constant work of the meek, gentle, and humble of heart.

*Blessed are they who hunger and thirst for justice; they shall have their fill.*

Who has never been a victim of injustice in this world? Our fragmentary vision of reality makes us all be unfair to one another. We want to be absolutely right in any issue without considering the opinions and reasons of others. Maybe others would contribute light to the same particular situation from a different point of view or a new angle we had neglected. Guilty or not guilty, we could be unjust in a determined situation. However, we recognized this unfairness only when we are the victims, never when others are the victims.

We create and develop unjust social and political systems, but usually we wash our hands not to recognize our complicity. It is not until we suffer an injustice committed against us, when we really understand injustice.

To feel hunger and thirst for justice means to live rightly, doing good daily. Christ is teaching us again to live consistently in an attitude of life committed in truth to love in action. This commitment means to work earnestly in pursuing a better world: The Kingdom of God.

Those who live in this attitude would eventually crash against injustice. Then, being victims, but thoroughly convinced of this true Christian ideal, they would have their fill. Those committed to keep looking for goodness, patiently and humbly, in the midst of injustice and ungratefulness, those will receive their fill, God's recompense for eternity. They would never fall into cynicism or despair. Christ will bless those who seek justice and truth. Do not worry or be afraid...Look at the lilies in the field! Blessed, happy are those who seek the Kingdom of God and its justice, everything else would be provided to them!

*Blessed are they who show mercy; mercy shall be theirs.*

The highest confirmation which shows a truly real human being in every culture and creed is *compassion*. Someone who is not compassionate cannot be truly a human being. Today, with the advances of psychology we can recognize and analyze the various traumas we human could suffer, either due to our genetic configuration or for our complicated situations due to our family, social, and psychological problems which affect each one of us. However, all of us deep down are called to be compassionate. We feel at peace with ourselves when we are able to give compassion and accept compassion.

Nevertheless, compassion could be obscured and even blocked by our selfishness. And the only way to get over this negative inclination, usually manifested in uncontrolled pride and cynicism, is to make an effort through sincere reflection. Compassion is not only a feeling, it is the result of effort, exercise on discernment, following the right choices and learning positively from the wrong ones. We would never be able to understand a way to happiness unless we can deeply comprehend the need to love and to be loved. Compassion is the true outward form of love. In the end, God himself will show us the fulfillment of his mercy. Blessed are they who show compassion, compassion shall be theirs.

*Blessed are the pure of heart for they shall see God.*

Purity of heart could be defined as clarity of conscience. King David turns to God asking him for *"a clean heart, and a resolute and generous spirit"* (Ps. 51: 12). However, Christ in this new dimension proclaims an attitude which destroys any kind of phariseism, or hypocritical self-righteousness. He was adamant against the attitude of the pharisees in his time.

As he constantly insists in the danger of the empty rule without the spirit, Jesus clarifies intensively that the true relationship between God and man, and the human beings with one another is based in love. In a loving relationship the purity of heart must be vital. It means a mutual trust that goes beyond human weaknesses and personal defects. Falsehood, lies, and deceit, cannot be in place in the pure of heart.

Jesus uncovered the sordid hearts of the pharisees trying to stone the adulteress. She had a clean heart after she faced Christ in shame in front of al these religious hypocrites. They, the pharisees, in contrast, did not possess a clean heart. One by one they dropped the stone and left. And Jesus, after they left, told her he did not condemn her either. What a tenderness contained Christ's final words to the woman! Go and sin no more. There is no threat, or warning – just a kind invitation.

Some may still be scandalized when reading the famous parable of the pharisee and the publican. Christ condemns the "religious" pharisee who goes to the temple to thank God for being so good. Being so good he despises sinners. When he prays, he could be ironically, like the model to many self-righteous Christians of today. Jesus, instead, contrary to our superficial expectations, praises the sinner publican, who humbly beats his chest praying God for forgiveness. The sinner had a clean heart, not the pharisee. The publican goes home happy and free in peace of mind. The pharisee goes back condemned in his own selfish pride.

It seems that to have a clean heart does not mean an achievement, something that could be seek and obtain with true effort and will power. A clean heart is an attitude. It means to follow a continuous process, a growing way of life which includes constant repentance and humble efforts to become better. By this process the individual discovers a clearer understanding of God's positive vision of life. No wonder Christ is blessing the pure of heart and promises them to be able to see God more and more without obstacles to the end in complete fulfilment of life. They shall see God, face to face!

*Blessed too are the peacemakers; they shall be called sons of God.*

Christ was announced by the prophets as *prince of peace* (Isaiah 9: 6) In a world of cruelty, oppression, and violence, his peaceful attitude claimed his own life. So today, in a world of social, economical, and political violence, with wars, terrorism, and unrest, this blessing of Jesus comes alive with a message of hope. Christ not only praises those who contribute to peaceful solutions and mediate between conflicting parts, he goes beyond to bless those who are promoters and "sowers" of peace.

The peace referred by Jesus is not a boring peace, the lack of war or conflict. Christ is talking about a dynamic and active peace, a definite product of justice put into practice. Christ announces an exciting peace created by a positive and actively brave love between all human beings. Jesus, the Prince of Peace blesses and rewards those who work for justice and peace. They will be recognized as children, sons and daughters of God.

*Blessed are those persecuted for righteousness and justice sake; the reign of God is theirs.*

It seems that persecution is the sign for the *chosen ones* both in the Old and the New Testament. The prophets had always been persecuted. Thus, the cross is the new sign for the Christians. Persecution will always appear when someone is fighting for justice and goodness. God's proximity is always rejected by those who, consciously or unconsciously, have chosen evil and death. The result for the just ones seems to be always: persecution. Joseph's envious brothers thought of killing him. Christ, rejected by his own, is sent to the cross. Selfishness and envy could provoke at times a violent reaction even from apparently good and respectful people.

In Jesus' life, his message and even his miracles provoked the most surprising reactions in the religious Pharisees and scribes. It is surprising to read how when Christ was healing a blind man, the narrow minded pharisees, oblivious of the good deed, just paid attention to the fact that it was done on Saturday when the Jewish law forbade to "work." The surrounding plain people, however, were marvelled at Christ. They recognized that Jesus really spoke with authority and conviction, not like the scribes and pharisees who kept repeating empty and ridiculous rules. These "religious" functionaries would not listen to Christ. Moreover, his words would burn their ears and hearts to the point of making violence against Jesus. He, though, had words of eternal life for those who listen.

True righteousness and justice seem to provoke the reaction of evil that always exists in this our incomplete creation. The forces of "Satan" are always present against goodness and against anyone who, like the prophets, keep denouncing evil and proclaiming hopeful love. However, Christ's blessing resounds till the end of times. Happy are those who suffer persecution for doing what is right and just: the Kingdom of God is theirs!

And Jesus Christ adds one more blessing for those his disciples of all time.

*Blessed are you when they insult you and persecute you and utter every kind of slander against you because of me. Be glad and rejoice, for your reward is great in heaven; they persecuted the prophets before you in the very same way.*

(Mt 5: 2- 12)

In the mystery of the incarnation of God, Christianity believes, all humanity already possesses Christ. So, all who in some way take Christ' attitude and his teachings of love in service of others, even though they might not have known or even have heard about Christ, these will share and enjoy these eternal blessings and rewards. (But Lord, when did we see you naked, lonely, or hungry...)

The beatitudes surprise us and mark a turning point in the history of humanity. These are not commandments; they are not rules or lists of rights or wrongs. These are blessings! The beatitudes disclose a new intimacy with God that goes beyond morality and ethics. Christ is speaking not even of religious principles, but something more profound. He is talking of deeply *human attitudes*, a true spirituality for the Christian, or better, a new way of being for every human: an ideal that becomes an ever growing task for anybody, a task that seems unlimited.

Christ's message in the Sermon on the Mount is anything but a sum of precepts. It deals with the imitation of Christ himself. Imitating him does not mean carrying out a number of regulations. There are good reasons why the Sermon on the Mount should open with promises of happiness for the unhappy. The gift, the present, and grace, are prior to the norm, the demand, the directive: everyone is called, to everyone salvation is offered, without any prior achievements. And the directives themselves are the consequences of his message of God's kingdom. His reaction is expressed only in examples and signs. If in Sinai the Jewish people accepted the Law as a loving gesture of God, now at the Sermon on the Mount humankind must joyfully receive this new dimension of God's love: Christ's message of the new covenant. *The beatitudes are the blessings for humanity, for every human being who is struggling and working through life to find one-*

*self, to find "the others", and to build the Kingdom as a fully realized human being.* Christ defines a "code" of directions for anybody who is always trying to become a better human being.

By the mystery of the incarnation, the *enfleshment* of God in all humanity we must realize that all humans already possess Christ deep in their hearts. All who follow Christ's attitude and teachings of love in service to others, even though they never even heard from Christ in their own worlds, they will receive these blessings. Therefore, they will be saved. Matthew explains this fact when Christ previews the last judgment and bluntly declares that whoever helped him (any of my least ones) was personally helping him. Surprised, these blessed ones will say, "but Lord, when did we see you naked, or hungry, or lonely, or sick…? These will share and enjoy their eternal blessings and rewards.

Jesus Christ expresses the beatitudes in a language full of love, compassion, understanding, and intimacy that is *way beyond the language of punishment and reward.* The Sermon on the Mount gives a new direction that includes every aspect of life, a realization of the ultimate spiritual integration*: self-donation in love.* In Sinai the law covered in primitive ways and language the relationship between God and man and between man and others, the vertical and the horizontal dimensions of man. The beatitudes speak in a language of love, in depths unthinkable by the Sinai standards.

The Sermon on the Mount, nevertheless, appears to state God's demands on humankind for the new covenant. The Sermon insists on *action.* Man himself must accept his responsibility in face of the closely approaching God. Hans Kung remarks: "In view of the ultimate and definite reality of the Kingdom of God a fundamental transformation is expected of man." John L. McKenzie declares that the beatitudes institute *a moral revolution that has not yet reached its fullness.* They are opposed to all conventional values of the Jewish and Hellenistic-Roman world and pronounce blessings on those who do not share these values. Not only the external values of wealth and status are repudiated but also those goods of the person that are achieved and defended by self-assertion and strife.

The beatitudes, in sum, are exalting the Suffering Servant as the model for humankind. The ideal of the Sermon on the Mount stands very high, so high that achieving it seems to be a never-ending task, which man would not be able to do by his own strength. It is certainly a call. *The response has to come from man by free choice, but the realization of that response also needs the help of God.* This understanding is terribly important for a clear comprehension of a true Christian Spirituality.

The Sermon on the Mount states Jesus' demands for humankind in the new covenant. Next come God's side of this new pact: Christ's self-sacrifice for humankind, the Suffering Servant, the Lamb of God. Christ's self-offering is considered to be the proof for all of us. We can imitate Christ in the beatitudes with the help of Christ himself. He has redeemed us, all humankind, through his death and resurrection.

## 20) THE GREAT CONTRADICION: DYING IN ORDER TO LIVE?
*The mystery of true happiness, according to Christianity.*

The hidden and the public life of Jesus offer abundant material for a true spirituality based on the imitation of Christ. It is his death and resurrection, nevertheless, that is considered the core of Christian spirituality. Christ's paschal mystery, as it is called, offers an explanation to the mystery of life and love and the purpose of life itself.

By the words at the last supper Christ reveals the mystery of redemption and the full realization of the Promise. *"This is the cup of my blood, the blood of the new and everlasting covenant. It will be shed for you and for all peoples for the forgiveness of sins."* By these words which have been used at the Eucharistic celebration for 2000 years, the meaning of the new pact was sealed, as something, not a symbolic instrument. When God makes the covenant with Abraham, the mark of his pact is the circumcision of every male: a pact of blood. In the new covenant it is the blood of Christ until the last drop as the gospels symbolically stress (John 19: 35). The blood of Christ would seal that eternal relationship between God and man. It is in the light of the paschal mystery that we can understand the meaning of the Sermon on the Mount and the *transcendental value of the beatitudes.*

We humans can barely understand the awesome mystery of Christ's purpose in life. But through a glance at Christ's life we may be able to understand our own purpose in life both individually and socially. Gilles Cusson explains that in dying, being judged, and condemned by the world which he is coming to save, and rising to life by the power of God, Christ is placed at the head of this new creation.

Christ is presented now in the same line traced by the Old Testament at the peak of Israel's maturity. Through centuries of evolution the yearning for the realization of the promise comes to an end in a new beginning that widens the vision to new consequences which have been announced by the Jewish writers, prophets, and priests. The new covenant opens up a new dimension, a new creation, but follows the same pattern and directions already lived throughout the history of Israel. Death, which seems to be the complete denial of life, is now transformed in Christ, into a way of unlimited life. *The negative is being transformed into the source of all positive.* Through all their process of growing, the people of Israel have believed in a God of life who ultimately defeats death. But nowhere before in the history of Israel do the Jewish people appear to understand the full meaning of this belief.

Nevertheless, the victory is not achieved through "magic" formulas, neither by denying death and the negatives of life, and definitely not by ignoring the consequences of evil and suffering. It is not a "Deus ex machina" who will solve in the Greek tragedies all the problems in an easy, almost expected, way from behind stage. *The victory of Christ is affirmed in the suffering acceptance of the human condition and its daily demands.* Christ's triumph is based on his humble acceptance of, or better, his faithfulness to God's design in creation. His trust in God will make him go through suffering and death itself.

That is the reason why Paul insists that only Christ and he crucified can be the real foundation for his message of life (1Cor. 3: 11)

(1Cor. 2: 2) The crucified Christ is the stumbling block for the Jews and an absurdity to the gentiles (1Cor. 22-25), but he is definitely the source of life, the power and the wisdom of God for all who are called to transcend.

At this point we have to realize that the theology of hope on which the whole Jewish tradition is based demands a deeper understanding. John Navone, S.J., in his work *A Theology of Failure*, declares: "The theology of hope with its emphasis on promises and the pull of a glorious future, requires a complementary theology of failure." By pure human standards, even by biblical Jewish standards, Jesus was a failure. Nevertheless, this apparent contradiction contains the most profound mystery in Christ's incarnation. Navone remarks that the historical failure of Jesus is a vitally important theological datum which renders Christian faith in the resurrection all the more remarkable and implies its trans-temporal character as a gift. Only faith can sustain that a man who died as a failure in the eyes of the world was a "success" before God.

As Jesus died, abandoned by his disciples (except John), he saw no evidence of his future community, comments Navone. This anxiety, linked to the fear of failure, appears in Jesus' agony in the garden of Gethsemane. Like all men, Jesus instinctively hoped to avoid the possibility of failure: he did not want to die. However, through the acceptance of the inevitability of his failure as an essential part of the divine plan, Jesus attained an inner peace beyond all human limitations. His overwhelming realization of his Father's love enabled him to *transcend his human fear of failure and death.* Through his awareness and experience of this love, Jesus revealed that the achievement of genuine human freedom is compatible with anxiety and crippling fears regarding the prospect of failure.

For Jesus, in fact, it is the hour of darkness. He is abandoned, according to Luke, to the triumph of darkness (Lk 22:53b). Jesus suffers in agony, *sharing a solidarity with every human being who is tempted to withdraw, to give up.* He knows there is not an easy way… *"Look! There is the Lamb of God who takes away the sin of the world!"* (John 1: 29)

*Jesus took Peter, John, and James*
*And he began to experience sadness and anguish.*
*Then he said to them:*
*"My heart is nearly broken in sorrow."*
(Mt 26: 37)

In spite of the unfaithfulness of man, beyond frustration, loneliness, and suffering, Jesus decides to stay with the Father in trust and fidelity. Unlike Adam, Christ humbly accepts God's design, God's call to risk and to trust. Like Abraham offers his own son and his future, Christ offers his own life and his future. Like Jacob who wrestles all night with the angel without prevailing, Christ does not prevail through the test. "Nevertheless, not my will, but yours be done." (Lk 22: 42)

Christ comes out of his test with the strength of God, carrying in silence the judgment of a world which condemns God to death en every age. He is the true Suffering Servant described by Isaiah. He will go to the cross with an inner peace that will exasperate forever those who condemn him. The shroud of Turin shows us a crucified man whose torture and painful death is marked all over his body. The face of that man, though, is paradoxically serene and peaceful.

John Navone offers a key comment that relates the mystery of the cross to the search of ultimate transcendence and happiness. "Through the mystery of the cross, Jesus has created a new perspective which frees us from the domination of the world as the ultimate source of human happiness." This world seems to drag us towards an animality that makes us slave of our instincts and our selfishness. *If the purpose of life is self-realization, self transcendence to the ultimate highest dimension, we must face and accept suffering, Christ's cross, in order to attain his ideal. There lies the real meaning of transcendence!*

If Christ opens for us the way to life and gives us the mean to follow that way, one thing stands very clear: he never forces us to follow him. Christ leaves us the ultimate responsibility to answer freely his call and invitation. The decision is up to us. A condition becomes a necessity: *"Whoever wishes to be my follower must deny his very self, take up his cross each day, and follow my steps."* (Lk 9: 23) At the same time we know what Christ affirms in the gospels: *"I am the light of the world. No follower of mine shall ever walk in darkness; no, they shall possess the light of life."* (John 8: 12) Such is the *Christian paradox*, affirms Cusson. We live individually and collectively the passion of Christ: that difficult passage individuals and societies go through from death to life. Nevertheless, the believer goes through the process in and with the light of Christ who is the true life.

The way is marked now with a profound realism. It seems that nobody can reach the ultimate Garden of Eden unless he first goes through the Garden of Gethsemane. The way opened by Christ in the future does not eliminate the tragic obstacle of evil and suffering. Nevertheless, human beings can learn to overcome all difficulties with an attentive and open disposition through dynamic discernment in faith and in hope. Jesus has overcome death and the power of evil. The Kingdom of God is indeed at hand!

According to Christian thinking, resurrection must come after the test of death. The individuals can find neither themselves nor the purpose of the universe unless they are tested. When all security is removed, when they have to face loneliness and death, then they understand. Like Christ every human being must go through death as the ultimate test. Like Christ, each one of us must trust. Christ is the confirmation of our constant series of tests which always result in new and deeper understandings. Resurrection is seen, then, as the logical follow-up of death. There must certainly be life after death, as there has been new life after every test we have experienced like "little deaths," from which new dimensions or new "lives" have resulted. It has been dawn after every night. It all seems to follow a logical pattern. Bluntly and clearly, in Christ the promise of life, although a mystery, becomes *eternal salvation and resurrection.* As Christ is the realization of the promise of salvation, he becomes, by his life, death, and resurrection, the fulfilment and total realization for every human being in eternal life. Therefore, man's purpose in life is more than *hominization;* it is real *divinization in Christ in an ultimate union with God.*

When Christ, after his resurrection, disappears from the world, he discloses the third reality of God's presence among us. Christ has already introduced the Father, the loving and faithful God of the Jewish people, by sending his disciples to the whole world. In Christ the mystery of the aspects (persons) of God is unfolded. He is the Alpha and the Omega, the beginning and the end. Christ is the pivotal point for understanding God's plan of salvation. Now the third person is introduced: The Spirit will lead humanity to the eschatological end and fulfilment.

*When the Spirit comes, however, being the Spirit of truth he will guide you to all truth...and will announce to you the things to come.*

(John 16: 13)

Christ's farewell has the same characteristics as Yahweh's previous reaffirmations of his presence through the Old Testament: *"And know that I am with you always until the end of the world."* (Mt 28: 20)


## 21) THE LORD OF FAILURE
*A redeemer and liberator who dies as a loser and a failure.*

The most extraordinary feature of the Christian tradition is the belief in a crucified God. Other traditions have described their gods in a wide variety of myths and ingenious conceptions. Man's quest for his creator and Supreme Being has led him to the worship of Mardouk, Zeus, and other grandiose images of gods. This multitude of gods usually possesses "man-made" characteristics which express the two extremes of human nature: either the perfection for which man yearns, or the evil and destructive force which man recognizes in his own self. The human mind can create the absolutely infinite god to whom man attributes order and authority. That supreme god is usually depicted as lacking understanding of human frailty and also remote and detached from his creatures. These creatures struggle, suffer, and die, almost ignored by the One who lives up there, contented in his own magnificence. Mardouk and Zeus can fulfil these characteristics.

On the other hand, the human mind can conceive evil gods to whom humans can attribute or even blame for all the negative things in life and for the evil inclinations in human nature. As in the Greek culture, man can also invent half-and-half gods who conform, too much, to humans in their weaknesses. Through these gods men may feel less guilty and more secure in the contradictions of life.

Even today humans still insist on creating new "ideal" gods. There is a tendency to conceive a god who is an absolute: beautiful, rich, successful and active. To this god, the so often dehumanized so called "successful man" of today can relate. We humans know, however, that we cannot ignore suffering, failure, injustice, poverty of all kinds, and death. In the face of war, greed, mass murders, and genocide, we cannot ignore our own frailty as victims and victimizers. We need to believe in a Superior Being, one way or another, in whom we can explain all this murky reality. "An absolute God would make us indifferent," declares Jürgen Moltman. "The god of action and success would let us forget the dead (referring to the wars), which we still cannot forget. God as Nothingness would make the entire world into a concentration camp."

Above all these man-made fabrications stands the Christian God, the crucified God. This is a God who does not ignore suffering, failure, injustice, or poverty because he is a God who has lived through that experience in his own flesh. A concept of God like the Christian God makes sense in the reality of the world. *This concept cannot be a human invention because it apparently denies every human instinct and desire of worldly self-realization.* The Christian God, paradoxically, still makes sense. It seems that we humans could have never invented a God who becomes man and shares man's misery. Without a special inspiration from that real Supreme Being himself, no one would have ever conceived a redeemer for man's misery who would come as a loser and would make himself a victim.

The Judeo Christian God reveals himself as the Lamb of God, the Suffering Servant of Yahweh, the crucified God. As Moltman says, he does not become Spirit, so that we humans would have to ascend into the Spirit to find God. He does not become simply the covenant partner of an elect people, so that one would have to belong to experience community with him. He humbles himself and assumes the whole and complete being of human reality, *so that everyone can share in him through his human existence*. The incarnate God is present and accessible to the humanity of every human being. No one needs to play a role or to transform oneself in order to come to his humanity through Christ. "I am who I am," alive and *present*, as he introduced himself to Moses. "I *am* with you always until the end of times," as he reassured his disciples when he left them in charge of his mission.

## 22) A UNIVERSAL MODEL FOR ALL HUMANITY
*A personal invitation to each one to complete the evolution.*

In his preaching Christ seems to continue the same message of life and hope given in the Old Testament. *He corroborates the main attitudes* already underlined and highlighted above when we studied the Old Testament. Thus Christ appears as the accomplishment of the promise: the new era about to begin. He signifies the completion of the old tradition, yet in a totally new light. Life is seen in the context of the *liberating love* of God that is now shared with human beings as friends and not servants. As if any doubt would still exist through all his "communications" in the past. God himself becomes human. This *enfleshment* of God produces a new acceleration in the process of humanity towards salvation and unification with God.

Jesus Christ, nevertheless, appears in an unexpected way. Isaiah and other prophets had already talked about him, yet he is not recognized. Just as the prophets predicted, he does not come as a ruler, not even as a social leader. He is not a success. He is a failure and a loser, humanly speaking. He is abandoned by his followers and even by his close friends when things start to go bad. He becomes man at the only level he can be identified by all humans, at the level of failure, loneliness, and suffering.

Like Job he is innocent. Like Job he is aware of and realistic about life. Christ confronts the threatening future like Jacob, even when he really knows that his decision will mean death. Christ is faithful to the end. He has the vision of total reality. The process of life in order to become a full person must include suffering and death. But *suffering and death lead to resurrection and real life.* His message, his teaching, now becomes clear.

Christ's hidden life already constitutes a statement. He lives thirty years as a regular simple human being, an "anawim." No one can overlook this extraordinary statement. Life, just life, living a regular daily life has a tremendous meaning for the Son of Man. He is already saving humanity at this point, just incorporating himself, God, into our human process. Therefore, *our simple life also has a saving power.* This was already previewed in the story of creation when Adam and Eve, all human beings, are created to be cooperators, co-creators with God. In Christ all of us are given the chance to *be co-creators with God just by living, working, suffering, growing, and hoping.*

Christ is boldly explicit when he indicates *he is the WAY,* and he shows us how that way is a continuous process of D*ecentration.* He makes himself very clear when he speaks. *The person must come out of oneself and live for others, get involved in the world and speak the truth in order to bring justice to the world.* Christ's message in his public life is blunt and even considered subversive. Yesterday, today, and always, his message crashes against our human nature and the destructive values all of us possess. That is why he becomes such a threat to the establishment. The pharisees and scribes definitely had to kill him and thus contributing to the final salvific element of the redemption mystery: the total sacrifice on the cross.

Through his death and resurrection Christ finally tells us the meaning of life. Gethsemane constitutes the ultimate temptation of

Christ, the moment when he must decide to accept death, paradoxically in order to gain life. After his anguishing acceptance *Jesus transforms suffering and death into the way to unlimited life.* He gives to the meaning of hope a new dimension far beyond the limits Job was able to convey. Christ's victory consists in the suffering acceptance of the human condition. On the cross, Christ is God of both the "upward" and the "forward." In his theory of evolution Teilhard de Chardin gives central importance to the meaning of the cross. The cross means *hard won victory, liberation, progress, saving power.* The road of the cross is no more and no less than the road of human endeavour supernaturally righted and prolonged. Teilhard adds with boldness that once we have fully grasped the meaning of the cross, we are no longer in danger of finding life sad and ugly. We shall simply have become more attentive to its barely comprehensive solemnity. Christ seems to be finally giving us the answer that has been hidden deep in the core of humanity and the process of life. The true meaning of the cross, of suffering, is *"towards progress through effort."* Suffering is the price of progress. We can present the cross to the world with enthusiasm, assures Teilhard, it should shock the loafers and the egoists; it should not be a scandal for those at the forefront of human progress.

Teilhard highlights an attitude of total abandonment in the unifying love as the true Christian attitude for life. But this abandonment must be characterized by active involvement in the world with the hope that gives ultimate meaning to life.

According to Teilhard's process of personalization the figure of Christ seems to bring the last stage, Super-centration, to a peak climax. Christ demonstrates in his own life, not only with words but also by the giving of himself to death for all, the ultimate purpose in life. Christ is the model, the ultimate fulfilment of the human being in love. He transcends life, through death into eternal life.

## CONCLUSION PART III
*A way of life for today's thinking human being.*

After analyzing the development of the Jewish positive vision that changed the world, we have encountered the controversial figure of Jesus. On studying Christ integrally with his message, we have found an attitude of life which his evangelists and followers proclaimed to the whole world as the way to find true happiness.

This spirituality or attitude of life, after all the historical movements in 2000 years, seems to have universal value for all humanity and for all times. This attitude of life brought by Christ's message is practically based on the mystery of the *enfleshment* of God. Through this mystery we get to understand that to be a Christian means to follow, to imitate Christ in his teachings and attitude. Our purpose in life, therefore, is intimately related to Christ's own purpose in life. When Christ becomes man, the universal human being is elevated to a new dimension of life. We are thus introduced to a new outlook of hope and are immediately incorporated into the acting love of God.

It is through Christ that the mystery of God unfolds before us human beings. Christ discloses three aspects of God through an audacious plan of salvation. God's revelation has appeared in three different persons during the evolution process of the history of salvation. God is explicated as one who unfolds into three persons: the Trinity. This doctrine of the Trinity is not an exorbitant and impractical speculation about God, declares Moltman, but it is nothing other than a shorter version of the passion narrative of Christ in its significance for the eschatological freedom of faith and the life of oppressed nature. If one conceives the Trinity as an event of love in the suffering and the death of Jesus, then the Trinity is no self-contained "group" in heaven, but the process for ultimate future fulfilment, which stems from the cross of Christ. This way of approaching the mystery of God is called "the economic Trinity," because it is studied from "our" human point of view, what matters to us: the practicality of the Trinity upon our personal lives. The Trinity is revealed to each one of us, the same way it is revealed in history.

God reveals himself to us personally in three different stages. This revelation unfolds from the central figure of Jesus. Christ introduces us to the Father and to the Spirit in what seems to follow three chronological stages in God's revelation to us humans. In these terms, we, time-thinking human beings with our limited understanding at least can grasp a basic awareness of God.

As a child trying to find our own identity and the world we live in, we usually perceive God as a Father, protector, and even authority figure. During adolescence we become more aware of the person of Christ. It is during this period of adolescence and young adulthood that we get truly concerned about "the others," our society, and about the problems of the world, Christ is the ultimate "other" with his social message, his personal relationship and even intimacy with us humans for whom he gives his own life: *"There is no greater love than this: to lay down one's life for one's friends."* (John 15: 13) In Christ man discovers his social responsibilities. I assure you, as often as you did it for one of my least brothers, you did it for me,… as often as you neglected to do it to one of these least ones, you neglected to do it to me.(Mt 25: 40, 45)

Finally, as mature persons, we are able to make a synthesis of the two previous aspects, the Father and Christ, and encounter the third aspect in our relationship with God: the Spirit who moves, enlightens, and inspires the universe and its people. Through this appreciation we are invited to "live" in the Spirit and help complete our own fulfilment and creation's fulfilment in service to the Kingdom of God.

Christian faith, therefore, becomes a personal relationship with God in his three persons or the three aspects in which we perceive him. The covenant, the pact of blood that God has made with all of us as humanity through the person of Christ, must *be understood in a deeply personal growing relationship.* The contact with the Father must help the individual grow in his self-identification process while developing a solid trust in the One who is always caring and present: "*I am who I am.*" A growing relationship with Christ helps the person find his brothers and sisters, his own place in society, and his responsibility in the triumph of justice: the working for the kingdom accepting his own cross and constant effort. *Life in the Spirit*, the third aspect of this relationship with God, must place the individual in true solidarity with all humankind in the role of co-creator with God. Life in the Spirit means sharing God's creativity in the flow of universal salvation and fulfilment.

We can courageously confront the obvious ambiguity facing us. On the one hand we have already been redeemed, liberated from evil by Christ's death and resurrection. On the other hand, we still live in this world and creation with all its negatives and growing pains. However, the Spirit, through inspiration and inner strength, will help us think, reflect, and discern day after day until the end of time.

The main feature in this relationship with God is our attitude of positive and active abandonment in him who is Father, Christ, and Spirit. This attitude has already been explained and studied in the Old Testament. We are to develop an active trust in God because he is always present and caring, mostly because he is above evil and has overcome suffering and death. Christian Spirituality, our practical way to live our faith, means, then, *life always in hope of life*.

Thus, the core of Christian spirituality, according to the Old and New Testament in the Bible, may be found in the idea of a personal encounter and active interaction with the Supreme Being. This encounter effectively includes a positive involvement with "the others" in service while being actively aware of the evolution and fulfilment of creation. What a fascinating and challenging adventure of life!

Christ's message of Christ is clearly directed to the mature struggling human being, searching for knowledge *centered* in oneself, *decentered* in others, and willing to *super-centered* in Christ, ultimate model and ideal, in that new dimension of love.

We have proposed Christianity as an answer to the purpose of life and consequently a true spirituality for the universal human being to attain that purpose as a way of life. We have explained how Christianity offers a theory of life that seems to be the only one that makes sense in the world today. Christianity has made even more sense since the appearance of the human sciences. The best proof, however, has been history alone. Only Christianity has survived the tests of time and history. It has even survived the narrow-minded cultural movements to which Christianity has been subjected.

After the initial outburst produced by Christianity in history, that included bloody persecutions by the Roman world, the persecutors themselves begin to assimilate this new and astonishing message.

Christianity became institutionalized during the Constantinean era, in the decadent period of the Roman Empire in the $4^{th}$ century. Thus it is accepted as the official "religion." Therefore, Christianity became identified with a particular civilization, losing its original impact. Even though Christianity has been, from time to time, defending its universal and transcultural value, this initial identification with the Roman Empire dimmed its powerful statement. Christianity became just "another religion."

Still, Christianity entering officially to the concert of the other major historical religions, brings us on the one hand, some similarities with them, but on the other hand, stunning differences. Hans Kung comments: "Not only Christianity, but also the world religions are aware of man's alienation, enslavement, need of redemption: inasmuch, that is, as they as they know of man's loneliness, addiction, abandonment, lack of freedom, his abysmal fear, anxiety, his selfish ways and his masks; inasmuch as they are troubled about the unutterable suffering, the misery of this unredeemed world and the sense and nonsense of death; inasmuch as they therefore await something new and long for the transfiguration, rebirth, redemption and liberation of man and his world… Not only Christianity, but also the world religions perceive the goodness, mercy and graciousness of the Divinity,"

Kung proceeds to declare *unfair, nevertheless, the comparison of Christianity with other religions.* Most of them have stopped developing and unable to adapt themselves to the changing times. There are enormous differences between Christianity and the religions of the world. Kung continues: "Hence, although the truth in other religions can be recognized, it cannot be disputed that there are substantial differences between the fearsome grimacing gods of Bali – the marvellous island of the gods - and a wall with icons of Orthodox saints in Zagorsk; between sacred temple prostitution and Christian consecration of virgins, between a religion whose symbol is the lingam (stone phallus), reproduced a thousandfold in the same temple, and another whose symbol is the cross; between a religion proclaiming a holy war against the enemy and a religion which makes love of enemies an essential part; between a religion of human sacrifice (at least twenty thousand human beings sacrificed within four days at the consecration of the main temple in Mexico in 1487 just when Cortes was landing) and a religion of everyday self-sacrifice for men. Even the cruelties of the Spanish conquistadores and the Roman burning of heretics –not in fact in accordance with the Christian scheme but contradicting Christ's teachings, not Christian but unequivocally anti-Christian– do not cancel out these differences.

Most oriental religions are heavily based on fatalism, unworldliness, pessimism, passivity, caste spirit, lack of social interest. For them it is difficult, almost impossible, to accept the reality of the world as it is today. Many believe in successive reincarnations, in which the "being" finds higher spiritual levels leading to a final happiness. However, psychology and sociology, among all the human sciences, strongly backed by common sense, argue such point of view. First of all, this "spiritual being" they propose, keeps taking successive different forms or bodies, with obviously different histories and genes, belonging to different society groups, even cultures. Family, friends, and relationships, are merely circumstantial. These human relationships are no other than passing shadows as the *Garuda Purana* claims. Therefore, the human beings are always without any real roots and become themselves passing shadows as well. Their personal and social interactions do barely count.

Moreover, this reincarnating-beings, never truly remember their previous reincarnations (unless like in some rich countries, they pay a usually expensive psychiatrist specialist in this sort of line). The reincarnating-being, they assure, keeps purifying itself, but never remembers previous experiences or errors. Therefore "it" can never truly learn through each life or stage. A human being deprived of personal characteristics would never find himself unless it happens on an ethereal spiritual level completely disconnected from reality. This reasoning denies one's true self identity and obscures the "ego" into a disfigured mass. In other words, it seems that we humans do not really exist.

But the worse and most dangerous issue of reincarnation lies in the lack of responsibility about society and "the others." Logically, individuals who believe everybody else is going through different and "better" levels of existence do not really care about their fellow human beings. This lack of social responsibility would obviously generate racism, and feed discriminating attitudes between social classes or castes. The truly reincarnated-being, it seems, does not care about injustices, world problems, and real universal human and material progress. If believers in reincarnation work for goodness, like many really do, this seems to be for pure self-perfection which makes them feel good. This attitude seems to foster selfishness and self righteousness, rather than a true sense of love in the service of others, something so deeply imbedded in our human consciousness.

Teilhard de Chardin declares that today every other religion is mercilessly halted in its development by the obstacle of a universe that has become so organic and so demanding that it outruns or disheartens most of the great mystical intuitions of the past. Christianity, however, rises effortlessly above this situation, carried along by the very conditions, so profoundly changed, of thought and actions to which the most eminent of its rivals cannot succeed in accommodating themselves. Christianity still makes sense in the world today and will always make sense because it is more than a mere religion. It is indeed transcultural and universal. It goes beyond the national and the patrimony of a particular culture. It has transcended time. Christianity is *a process and a way of life for all times*. These were the *good news* preached by the first apostles to the whole world.

However, as we had said, its universal and transcultural character was thus diminished by the Greco- Roman emphasis of the Emperor Constantine, which even clouded its original oriental character. Christianity suffered greatly during its successive development, when the Church's spiritual power was sought by the powerful political forces of the Middle Ages as an instrument to impose political dominion.

From then on, Christianity keeps growing painfully. Each epoch would apply the gospel attitude through a changing and evolving world. But through all these changes and stages, it is always stays clear that Jesus has been the seed planted by the Father to germinate and grow. The Spirit *evolving in time,* would make the world understand this message and its mystery through the centuries until the end of time.

For 2000 years, great prophets and holy women and men have spread the gospel. Their work and mission have kept the Church moving and growing. Key to this historical process has been saints like Francis of Assisi, who with his evangelical poverty and simplicity inspired the Renaissance and restored evangelical Christianity after centuries of medieval obscurantism. Catherine of Siena and Theresa of Avila helped restore the true spirit lost in the midst of historical confusion. Ignatius of Loyola, with his Spiritual Exercises, offered his method of spirituality to all renaissance modern human beings then and now. This method which facilitates a true personal encounter with God, helps the questioning men and women to commit themselves to the kingdom of love, justice and peace, through Christ's attitude taught in the gospels.

Recently, Mother Theresa of Calcutta had been a living testimony of the Christian message to all races, religions, and cultures. Quietly, but intensely she showed us what the beatitudes of the sermon of the mount really mean. She preached the message in action by lovingly caring and helping the suffering and abandoned. All through our tempestuous history, these saints and prophets keep restoring and nourishing the true Christian attitude, by rediscovering Christ as the main center of life and the universe.

Christianity is much more than a fixed system, says Teilhard, presented to us once for all, of truths which have to be accepted and preserved literally. For all its resting on a core of *revelation*, it represents in fact a spiritual attitude which is continually developing; it is the development of a Christic *consciousness* in step with, and to meet the needs of, the growing consciousness of mankind.

In summary, *Christianity gives us the answer to life, a true spirituality, a way to attain our purpose in life and true happiness. It is certainly a universal, transcultural, and a valid way for all times because it is rooted in general basic human attitudes that through the centuries have been proven to be universal.* Christianity goes beyond morality and sociological systems: it can be accepted by any individual, whatever the nature or the level of his "call." It is a call to life and every human being shares this call to total realization.

Christian Spirituality is a valid method for living with and through the purpose in life. It is definitely supported by the human sciences: psychology, sociology, philosophy, and history, and based on a true solid theology. Christian spirituality is a way of life through attitudes of living in faith, hope, and love to a total realization. Its key feature is our personal relationship with God in his three persons, Father, Son, and Holy Spirit, as each one of us goes through our own process of personalization. Christian Spirituality could definite give meaning to the world today. Moltman offers us a radical and brilliant conclusion to his study on Christ, the Crucified God:

"Our officially optimistic society believes in the idols of action and success. Through their compulsive inhumanity, they lead many persons into apathy and despair. The churches in this society often function as nothing more than religious establishments, care-takers for the idols and laws of this society. If this society is to turn itself toward humanity, the churches must become Christian. They must destroy the idols of action and apathy, of success and anxiety; proclaim the human, the suffering, the crucified God; and learn to live in this situation. They must discover the meaning of suffering and sorrow, and spread abroad the spirit of compassion, sympathy and love. They must confront the successful and despairing man with the truth of the cross in his situation, so that man *may become compassionate, joyous, and thereby free being.*"

Christian realism is based on hope, but a hope in life as it realistically presents hardship and struggles. Christianity aims definitely at the future like a truly theory of life which invites us to bring it down to earth and put it into practice.

The universal Christ will be known more and more as the only answer, the way to find happiness. The crucified Christ, triumphal Jesus, will finally be known by all nations, all races and cultures. Christ the liberator and redeemer will be recognized by all and each one who either follow him or seek him with sincere heart. Christ will be known as internal and personal strength, but also as social force toward justice and harmony. He is and will be the source of a universal evolution toward the plenitude of eternal happiness.

# EPILOGUE

In the pursuit of happiness we have found a purpose of life that seems to make universal sense today as it did when it first made an appearance in antiquity. The positive vision of the Jewish people recorded in the Bible out ruled all other interpretations in times of the Roman Empire when a universal idea of humanity was being conceived. This positive unique vision unthinkable for those times, set the human being as an agent of an extraordinary future destiny, both incomprehensibly and grandiose. It brought a hopeful dawn for all humanity in universal creation. Today there is no other comparable view of life.

Searching for happiness we have also found a way evolving through history that also makes sense in our vision of the future. This way shows a human being growing in awareness of a desired but apparently impossible freedom. Human beings appeared in ancient cultures as the victims of oppressive cultures and their gods. This newfound way strongly opposes all oppressive systems that men, blinded by their own selfishness, and making themselves into gods, impose on others.

In our pursuit of happiness, we stumbled into a complete different God, who was not like those who subjected the human beings purposelessly to suffering and death. This God, encountered little by little through a *graced* evolution in consciousness, is a God of life who challenges humans to be responsible and to face reality and future with courage and serenity. He is the God of justice, but at the same time, a friend and personal God who cares for each one of us. This God invites and inspires us without either coercing our freedom, or blocking our individual creativity. This concept of God could have never been invented or created by us humans.

From the very beginning this God revealed a mysterious promise which would be disclosed, even developed, in time. This promise reassures the human being with a hopeful future for the individual, society and universal creation. However, by the revelations from that God, his interaction with the people who discovered him, and our own present experience, we become aware of a negative factor we human have to deal with. Our human selfishness keeps hurting the graced relationship between God and ourselves. We remain bound to the negativity of our selfishness. This appears to be the universal problem for all times. The ambiguity we encounter is based in our own freedom. Human beings can choose and decide between good and evil, two constant forces pulling us in opposite ways. These forces, unfortunately, are never present as a "black and white" reality. In being so, it would be easy for a mature person with an educated consciousness to make the right decisions. Unfortunately most problems arrive in a "grey" and foggy tone. The human being must, then, make a constant effort to develop consciousness even in a daily basis. Our process of growing in consciousness is a never ending task.

We have already experienced many social and political systems in our world history. Each one had tried to offer universal solutions, usually under arrogant and absolutists tones. Too many of them mount to philosophical theories up in unrealistic platitudes. One by one they keep crumbling to the ground. All of them seem to fall short of finding a real solution, maybe because they have forgotten their principal subject: the human being created by God for self-transcendence. Perhaps we will never find an ideal system. However, we certainly shall not find any good system which neglects the transcendental necessities of the individual human being. Only from the human being as that point of departure we would be able to provide with new social and political, and even economical systems to solve the universal problems of humanity.

Many religions have also made that mistake of considering the individual as an object that must obey without thinking or questioning. Christianity itself had fell several times in history into this temptation, truly against the spirit of freedom and respect of personal dignity proclaimed by God himself and taught by Jesus.

In the evolving historical development we just have followed, we finally reached that incredible fascinating figure of Jesus. For all times, the promise given to the Jews for humanity became a reality in history "in the fullness of time." He came with a unique impact arriving to us today as the only answer that makes sense in a world of inhumanity, loneliness, and anguish. Although we know, this destructive element will always be present in our human nature, the figure of Christ will always proclaim the greatness of the human being, thinker, creative, and collaborator of God in the progressive evolution of creation. Moreover, Christ is the end and completion of this evolution of which he was also the beginning.

Christ came unexpectedly, even though he had been announced for centuries with these particular characteristics. Instead, his own people expected him in a different way, in "human way," in the narrow minded level of success and power. Thus his own, all enslaved by world selfishness, rejected him. Christ came humble, to give instead of to receive. He came to forgive rather than to judge and to condemn. History interpreted him in many human ways, but Christ has always "survived" as the mysteriously divine seed planted by God, and germinating in each and all human beings.

An astonishing renewal in history occurred right after the Middle Ages. The Renaissance constituted one of those rare periods in history, a climax of culture which spread and developed to shape the modern world even to our days. This turning point in history began with the figure of Saint Francis of Assisi, around 1200 A.D. He preached simplicity of life in times of opulence and luxury that blurred the clarity of the gospels in the Church. His love for nature brought all the artists of the times to look deeply into the beauty of God's creation and the uniqueness of the human being. Francis of Assisi inspired a renewed evangelical spirit centered in Christ's teachings.

The Renaissance was understood not only as a cultural historic period in which humanistic values were reborn through creative expressions of art.

Furthermore, the Renaissance period marks a true rebirth of lost human values in the historical progress interrupted by the barbarian invasions in Europe. The human being, the most perfect work made by God, becomes the center of the universe, the perceiver and questioner of everything in the universe, including himself. Science, art, political systems, faith and religion, all coincide to re-establish the human being and his universe as point of departure of this new epoch.

The whole world was changing. Guttenberg had just invented the printing press. For the first time in history people could read history and the Bible among other works of literature. The classical Greco-Roman world was rediscovered and literally unearthed from the Roman ruins. Plato, inspirer of a philosophy based in the fundamental questions of man, was rehabilitated and studied. The discovery of America for Europe, brought a completely new vision of the world and the Universe. Astronomy and the new sciences changed the fixed laws of universal order and a vast infinite opened up in unlimited cosmic proportions. The Renaissance was really an extraordinary twist in history: a new beginning.

In the midst of these revolutionary changes, in 1491, Ignatius of Loyola was born in Spain. A warrior, and a noble gentleman full of pride and vanity, he experienced a conversion after being wounded in the battle of Pamplona. While recovering he changed his life radically and dramatically. Leaving everything behind, he decided to follow God by helping others.

During these changes Ignatius left us a remarkable document, his Spiritual Exercises, in which the individual can follow a method to encounter God and begin an intense personal relationship with him. Loyola's Spiritual Exercises integrate, for the first time, one's own psychological movements into a personal Christian Spirituality based on the Bible. Ignatius used his own experiences dealing with the mundane world of the Renaissance. But mostly he studied his own internal moods and inspirations through his conversion. His efforts to fight the apathy of the times failed several times. Like all prophets, ahead of his time, he suffered persecution. Ignatius was imprisoned by the Inquisition, accused of writing dangerous spiritual theories. The Spiritual Exercises were confiscated and meticulously analyzed. However, with his deep realistic knowledge of Europe with its social and political, especially religious confusion, he was able to understand and clarify the role of the renewed "Renaissance Man" as an agent and collaborator of God in creation.

Ignatius of Loyola experienced in his own life the changes from the Middle Ages to the modern world of the Renaissance. From a medieval gentleman and a warrior, he became a true renaissance man through his conversion, his studies in Salamanca and Alcala, and finally at the university of Sorbonne in Paris, center of the then "dangerous" humanist theories. Ignatius lived and suffered the corruption and division of the Church. Ignatius lived the times of Lorenzo of Medicis, Machiavelli, and Emperor Charles V in whose reign the sun never set. He read the writings of Savonarola and Erasmus. Ignatius suffered the corruptions of the Church Luther was so vehemently denouncing. Nevertheless, Loyola kept faithful to the Church and worked with others for a reformation from within.

In Rome, Ignatius of Loyola founded the Society of Jesus, the Jesuits, a new and dynamic religious order, unique in its approach and vitality in those tempestuous times. He wrote the Jesuit Constitutions that gave a body to that renewed Christian spirit. The Jesuits went all over the world preaching and teaching the gospel. The Jesuit missions announced the "good news" respecting the dignity of the people and their cultures, but also bringing progress to their lives. This eventually clashed with the political powers of the times and caused the suppression of the Jesuit order for many years.

To the poor house where Ignatius of Loyola lived in Rome the last years of his life, came princes, cardinals, and religious notables to ask for spiritual help and advice. Some came listen to the Gospels for the first time, when unfortunately many religious authorities lead a life far from the teachings of Christ. Some followed his Spiritual Exercises and received this remarkable method of life to integrate in themselves a new total and true vision of Christianity.

## A METHOD TO FIND THE WAY TO HAPPINESS

Ignatius of Loyola elaborated a method to find one's own purpose of life. He knew well that in order to change his confused world in turmoil, the starting point was to change the individual. From this basis, they could begin the new desired society. With a strength and conviction parallel to that of the first Christians, Ignatius offered that new born world the same message the apostles had brought fifteen centuries before. It was a refreshing way to announce salvation to all nations, after Christianity had been through the deep crisis of the Middle Ages. The barbarians almost destroyed European culture. This destruction unleashed greed and the ambition of powerful feudal families who used Christianity to oppress and politically control the new forming nations.

To that world Ignatius of Loyola brought his Spiritual Exercises offering a new spirituality. The new apostles, men and women, would be contemplatives in action, truly centered in Christ and committed to his teachings.

Ignatius opens his Spiritual Exercises with the Principle and Foundation, based on the Bible and following the history of salvation. This first "exercise" was basically the understanding of the purpose of life for each individual. Created by God, with a mission that covers it all, including one's own person, the human being must order his life aiming for a glorious universal end. The way to follow must be to work with others and establish the kingdom of love announced by Christ. Ignatius seems to stress the responsibility of all Christians to put their faith into action. However, Ignatius points out, the individual is free to follow this growing process of life. The human beings must not deny, but accept their humanity. They are invited by God to rightly use everything in creation, but only as far as (*tantum quantum*) this helps them to procure the ultimate end to which we had been created.

Thus Ignatius leads the individual to a personal encounter with God, who has revealed himself in history as living and loving God. This is a God, who is faithful to his powerful evolving creation which he moves from within. The human beings created by God in his own image, are free to choose between good and evil. They could even be unfaithful to their own creator by rejecting the same end to which they had been created. Therefore, human beings ironically can even reject their true and final happiness.

Just there, Ignatius uncovers the danger to which every human being is prone and vulnerable by his own nature. Humans by their own selfish nature can become inhuman and thus create oppressive reactions, individually and socially, against God's gentle invitation to collaborate with him. We human beings could outrageously misuse our destiny if we let our selfishness unleashed. Ignatius knows our sinfulness very well and insists on accepting it humbly, as the only way to begin over powering this negativity Set in this awareness, the Christian can now build a realistic hopeful attitude in life. Christ has overcome sin. We must join him and trust.

After the initial discovery of the Principle and Foundation, Ignatius takes the individual through series of steps. Meditations, reflections and prayer, help the individual following the Spiritual Exercises grow in consciousness and become aware of his or her destiny. All this is integrated with the personal encounter with Christ and his message. At first, this integration takes place by getting to know Christ, his life, his practical message, and his mystery. Then, the individuals are invited to identify themselves with Christ, even in communion with him, through the mystery of his death and resurrection. They must sincerely test their own realistic dispositions. Ignatius offers a series of "elections" or decisions to be pondered much deeper each time. The purpose is to help the individuals commit themselves to the attitude of life clearly described and taught by Christ in the gospels. The attitude is to follow Jesus by giving oneself to all others in love in service.

When the individuals following the Exercises are able to understand this higher and intense step, they are to be reborn into a new dimension called by Loyola: *life in the Spirit.* The person is now in the hands and guidance of the Holy Spirit.

The method elaborated by Ignatius of Loyola seems to be as actual today as it was 500 years ago. It seems to be transcultural and universally valid for all times, especially in our confused world of today desperately needing a purpose and a hopeful definite goal.

As we have followed in our study, according to the Judeo-Christian tradition, the human beings are not fatalistically condemned to evil and death. Human beings, on the contrary, are destined to grow in consciousness and to evolve in creation.

Martin Descalzo tells us that we could have become aware of our great role and responsibility just with the account on creation. However, in this new message brought by Christ, our destiny is far greater, for the particular reason of *what we could possibly become*. Our capacity to become active members of the Kingdom of God and our capacity to become new creative human beings, constitute our most greater gift. The gospels shouts full of joy a personal and global invitation to risk, to jump into the challenging unknown, to progress and get more involve in this fascinating life.

And Ignatius of Loyola provides us with the method to exercise our spirit and to find freely, the great destiny awaiting us. This destiny must be pursued bravely but at the same time, with humble simplicity. The new apostle becomes integrated to a true realistic mission of love: *a contemplative in action*. Ignatius' method, have lead us to a total liberation in God. It is a way for us all to get rid of the "idolatry" of ourselves and our possessive material things. Because we human beings, narrow minded and blind, can refuse to accept the best of our human condition and choose to become slaves of money, power, pleasure, and crippling selfish interests. We have a tendency to make things –that are merely means—into foolish and unworthy ends. Apparently we prefer to renounce freedom and regress to "the safety" of our animal instincts.

Christ fails with the rich young man who prefers to be rich than to become free (Mt 19: 16). On the contrary, Christ redeems Zacheus, who only when he renounces to his riches, he acquires human stature (Lk 19: 5). Jesus offers his invitation, but we are free to follow him or reject him. Christ allows us to make the final personal decision.

Ignatius through his Spiritual Exercises helps us find and encounter this Christ, the liberator, with the message, the attitude of life he came to show us as the true way. Loyola leads us to discover that new world which we are invited to build. However, he evidently knows, we are the ones who must freely make the decision to follow Christ's way of life, his kingdom of peace.

The Spiritual Exercises explain how Jesus saves us from the false gods we keep inventing and keep accosting us through our lives. Nevertheless, despite internal or external evil forces we do receive the reassurance from this God who is salvation and complete happiness: "I am with you, I will be with you until the end of times."

---

Maybe our readers have already become aware that explaining and developing the itinerary of this work about the pursuit of happiness, we have been following the logical itinerary of the Ignatian Exercises. We have departed from the individual as the subject. We have inquired the fundamental questions asked by any human being in the world today, and maybe in any time in history. We have inserted ourselves into the historical context of the Western civilization. We have investigated the reasons why our Western world has found certain answers through the ages, valid for all humanity. The dynamic and evolving history of our world we have followed has given us the real framework to find our Principle and Foundation. We have discovered the God of a positive vision, salvation, and happiness. The Jewish written tradition made by group and personal reflection through doubt, failure, faith and unfaithfulness, has come to us in the Bible as a unique manual to find answers.

The history of Israel has conducted us to Jesus, the Christ, who liberates us from the obstacles preventing us from becoming fully human, realized, and therefore, from finding true happiness. After following this development of our search for happiness, it seems we are urged to make a transcendental decision in life. The Spiritual Exercises of Ignatius of Loyola incite us to take a stand.

In response to this stunning challenge, we reach the transcendental levels announced by Pierre Teilhard de Chardin, who has transported us to a higher level of life in the Spirit: the cosmic future of the total realization in Christ, the Alpha and the Omega, the ultimate universal evolution. This is the inviting and serene field of Christ's kingdom described by Ignatius. In Christ each one of us is called to be an agent of transformation: the resplendent mission of being light of the world and salt of the earth. To the daring we recommend the Ignatian Exercises for putting into practice our graced discovery of the way to happiness.

## NOTE

The theme developed in this work is the written material of the doctoral thesis of its author after his studies at the Pontifical Gregorian University in Rome. This thesis, directed by Fr. Gilles Cusson, S.J., was defended and awarded a Magna Cum Laude in 1985.

This thesis grounded the core and the spirit of a unique mission of service in the Dominican Republic, which a group of young Jesuits designed and develop since 1973. The ILAC Mission integrates spiritual commitment and love in service to all in need, rich or poor. On the one hand ILAC offers multiple programs to the people of remote rural areas of the Dominican Republic. These programs, designed to develop their rural communities, include the improvement of their health, education for the adult, especially the women, the training of leaders. The success of these programs has encouraged the ILAC Mission, to embark into more projects and programs related to their agricultural possibilities, and cultural development in general.

On the other hand, hundreds of foreign volunteers have participated as volunteers. Health care professionals, educators, builders and constructors, and thousand of students and professionals, keep benefiting from a unique learning spiritual experience while they offer their needed service. All participants, those who offer the service and the ones who receive it, follow the itinerary of the Ignatian Exercises as a help to experience a deep transformation in life. This dynamic interchange of loving service has produced over the years abundant fruits of life and hope. After more than thirty years, the "campesinos" themselves develop and run these programs with serious responsibility and exemplar dedication. Their quality of life materially and spiritually has improved immensely. Their dignity, commitment to love in service and joyful attitude, certainly constitutes a learning experience for the foreign volunteers who come to serve from different countries and cultures, in a true commitment of love. Local professionals and influential Dominicans also participate and support these programs with their own courageous personal involvement.

All of them together work to help one another through this "humanizing" spiritual mission. The whole experience is based in the spirituality of the Bible, both the Old and the New Testament, and truly inspired by the Spiritual Exercises of Ignatius of Loyola. This spirituality invites all who participate whatever their religious faith is, to commit themselves with fire and passion to the universal message and attitude of life taught and lived by Jesus the Christ. This seed, sown by him, is spread through the whole world quietly and humbly by all who believe in a loving God who sends us to serve and help one another.

# PRINCIPAL BIBLIOGRAPHIC SOURCES

Anonymous. *Gilgamesh,* A verse narrative by Herbert Mason, A Mentor Book, New American Library, New York, 1972.

Cahill, Thomas, *The Gift of the Jews*, Doubleday, New York, 1998.

Cusson, S.J,, Gilles. *Notes d'Anthropologie Biblique*, Institut de Spiritualitè, Universitèe Gregorienne, Rome, 1977.

_____, *Un Jardin en Eden nommè Gethsemane*, Cahiers de Spiritualità Ignatienne, Quebec, 1978.

_____, *Conduis-moi sur le Chemin d'Eternitè*, Les Editions Bellarmin, Montrèal, 1973.

_____, *Pedagogie de l'Experience Spirituelle Personnelle*, Les Editions Bellarmin, Montrèal, 1968.

Grant, Michael. *The World of Rome*, A Mentor Book, New American Library, New York, 1969.

Haag, Herbert. *Is Original Sin in Scripture?* Sheed and Ward, New York, 1969.

Hauser, Arnold. *A Social History of Art*, Vintage Books, New York, 1961.

Kasper, Walter. *Jesus the Christ*, Paulist Press, New York, 1976.

Kung, Hans. *On Being a Christian*, Double day and Company, Inc., New York, 1974.

_____, *The Catholic Church, A Short History*, A Modern Library Chronicles Book, The Modern Library, New York, 2003.

Loyola, Ignacio, *Autobiografía-Ejercicios Espirituales*, Aguilar, Madrid, 1961.

Martin Descalzo, Jose Luis, *Jesús de Nazaret*, Ediciones Sigueme, Salamanca, 2000.

Moltman, Jurgen, *The Crucified God*, Harper and Row, New York, 1974.

_____, «The Crucified God», *Theology Today*, April, 1974.

Navone, S.J., John, *A Theology of Failure*, Paulist Press, New York, 1974.

Teilhard de Chardin, S.J., Pierre, *Christianity and Evolution*, Harcourt Brace Jovanovich, New York, 1971.

_____, *Toward the Future*, Collins St. James' Place, London, 1975

*The Interlinear Greek-English New Testament*, Samuel and Sons, Ltd., London, 1960.

*The New American Bible*, Thomas Nelson Publishers, Catholic Publishers, Inc., New York, 1971.

*The New Jerusalem Bible*, Doubleday, New York, 1999.

www.ingramcontent.com/pod-product-compliance
Lightning Source LLC
Chambersburg PA
CBHW070142080526
44586CB00015B/1807